Date Due

7-13-99			
MAR 17 '99			
APR 08 '99			
MAY 06 '99			
OCT 22 '99			
MAY 06 '00			
SEP 5 '00			
OCT 7 '00			

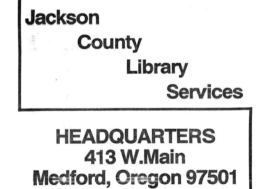

A Celebration of
AMERICAN DOLLS

from the
Collections of
Strong Museum

by Dorothy A. McGonagle

Ellen M. Manyon
Curator of Recreational Artifacts,
Strong Museum

Darlene Gengelbach
Doll Conservator, Strong Museum

Donald Strand
Photographer, Strong Museum

Published by

Hobby
House
Press
™

Hobby House Press, Inc.
Grantsville, Maryland 21536

Dedication

For Jerome,
in loving memory of my parents, George and Mary Cairns, whose strong values encompassed my childhood,
and to the memory of Margaret Woodbury Strong, whose legacy has but begun to be felt.

Acknowledgements

I would need to write another book to adequately thank all those who have supported my efforts in the creation of this one. First and foremost, my handsome and good husband, Jerome, my partner, who should share authorship, was as always my anchor and my espouser. He is also the artist behind the several charming drawings for this book. A few good women gave of their friendship and expertise in ways too deep to enumerate, notably my esteemed colleagues, June Prescott Kibbe, Agnes Sura, Janet Hollingsworth, Maurine Popp and Margaret Whitton, who initially introduced me to the wonders of the Strong Museum when she was their first doll curator. Gratitude is extended to current Strong Museum personnel Kathy Castle, Ellen Manyon, Darlene Gengelbach and Jean Banker who unlocked cases, revealed dolls high and low, provided mountains of print-outs from which I worked and facilitated some unique requests in readying dolls for the museum photographer, Don Strand and his volunteer assistant Bill Tribelhorn. Strong Museum Librarian Carol Sandler's cheerful willingness to make research materials available during my tenancy in her side "office" is greatly appreciated. Other museums and their representatives who assisted in rounding out a few areas include Rosalie Whyel and Susan Hedrick of the Rosalie Whyel Museum of Doll Art in Bellevue, Washington; Nancy Roper of the Kendall Doll Museum, Lorna Lieberman for Wenham Museum, and Pamela Zampiello for the Concord Museum, all in Massachusetts. Other good friends also graciously allowed the use of their historically significant dolls, especially Phyllis Kransberg and Marilyn Johnson, Rebecca M. Brignoli, Rebecca Mucchetti, Jayme and Brooke Ward and Claire Castle, as well as Ursula Mertz and Nancy and Dave Carlson, fellow authors, who, like the following, affably answered questions in their specialties: John Axe, Dorothy and Jane Coleman, Carol Corson, Judith Izen, Winnie Langley and Dorothy Dixon, Glenn Mandeville and Cynthia Musser. I tender sincere thanks to many of these friends who also read the manuscript in progress and offered suggestions, and to the following, who also provided their highly valued input and their myriad forms of support: Loretta Akers, Lyn Brignoli, Faith Eaton, Patricia Gosh, Naomi McGovern, Penny Phelps, Jim and Ronnie Robison, Zick Rubin, Suzi Smith, Toni Stephan, Fred Sura, Leonard Swann, and most notably historian Richard Lyman, PhD. Harvard, whose close attention to the text from his specialty of childhood history is deeply appreciated. This commitment underscored that the greatest measure of wealth is friendship. As always the support of my family, particularly my three children and their spouses, was extraordinary and multi-leveled, from sharing their doll play memories as part of the foundation for writing to reading and rereading text, to cooking and cleaning when I wasn't...I couldn't have done it without them! And it couldn't have been done without the resolution of the publisher, Gary Ruddell and his staff, and the editor, Mary Beth Ruddell, who understood and faced the challenge of producing so complex and wide-ranging a book.

Note: Strong Museum's registration numbers for each doll are supplied as a reference for readers' questions.

Consultant
Jean M. Burks, *Curator of Decorative Arts*, The Shelburne Museum, Shelburne, VT

Front Cover: Proudly American stand these three early 20th century cloth dolls: Martha Chase's George Washington, Ella Smith's Alabama Indestructible Doll and Georgene Averill's "Miss America", seen also on page 103.
Title Page: Ives' "Daughter of the Regiment", c. 1876, celebrates the country's centennial. See also page 69.
Back Cover: A sampling of American dolls surround a folk art 48 star American flag comprised of hundreds of red, white and blue buttons sewn to a cardboard backing and framed (76.2711) constructed some time between 1912-1959, its maker remains unknown. The dolls, also seen in their respective sections are, clockwise from top left, a lovely papier-mâché Lerch lady and a cloth Izannah Walker, 19th century treasures; a wooden Schoenhut girl, Effanbee's composition Patsy and Mattel's plastic Barbie® doll, classic 20th century American dolls.

About the Author

Dorothy McGonagle has been collecting and researching antique dolls for 25 years. She lives with her husband, Jerome, and a few cats in Sudbury, Massachusetts. Long-time contributing members of UFDC (United Federation of Doll Clubs), she and Jerome were the 1995-1997 Associate Editors—Antique Dolls, for the UFDC quarterly, *Doll News*. Together they present the acclaimed UFDC Traveling Seminar, "French Bebes". Dorothy is also past president of the Yankee Doodle Dollers of Massachusetts and the Doll Collectors of America. She is the author of the Hobby House book, *The Dolls of Jules Nicolas Steiner*, and is the American Consultant and contributing photographer for the forthcoming London publication *Dolls* by Olivia Bristol. She has lectured extensively on a wide range of dolls and doll related topics all across America, in Europe and in Australia, bringing her love of dolls and the stories they tell through the generations of children who played with them to her audiences with her vision and inimitable style. She holds a Bachelor of Arts degree in English Literature from Boston University, and is the mother of three married children and one dynamite grandchild — to date.

Additional copies of this book may be purchased at $29.95 (plus postage and handling) from
Hobby House Press, Inc.
1 Corporate Drive
Grantsville, Maryland 21536
1-800-554-1447
or from your favorite bookstore or dealer.

©1997 Hobby House Press

ISBN: 0-87588-479-2

TABLE OF CONTENTS

INTRODUCTION

by Ellen M. Manyon
Curator of Recreational Artifacts
Strong Museum

The Strong Museum manages the world's largest public collection of dolls.

Strong Museum is proud to present wonderful highlights from its vast collection of American dolls. As a history museum charged with the mission to interpret everyday American life, dolls can be used to reveal the tastes, fantasies, sensibilities and style unique to this country. From primitive wood to hard plastic dolls, and from Izannah Walker to Xavier Roberts, this book will cover many of the materials and manufacturers of those distinctly American dolls.

Strong Museum's collection all began with Margaret Woodbury Strong. Born in 1897, she was the only child of John Charles and Alice Motley Woodbury. The Woodburys became investors in the Eastman Kodak Company. With their discretionary income, they travelled the world with their little girl.

While on these trips, Margaret Woodbury developed a penchant for collecting anything that fascinated her. When she married Homer Strong in 1920, she had inherited quite a fortune. Their only daughter, Barbara was born in 1921, and soon after the family moved into a 50 room estate just outside of Rochester, NY. After the death of her daughter in 1946, and her husband in 1958, Mrs. Strong dedicated her life to collecting.

From dishes to dolls, Mrs. Strong amassed a collection of over half a million objects, most of which reflected the material culture of American middle class life from 1820 on. When she died in 1969, she wanted a museum to be created that would showcase her collection so that others could share in her delight with fascinating things.

In 1982, Strong Museum opened as an educational institution charged with the mission to interpret American life since 1820 with an emphasis on social issues and popular culture. The museum was also charged with the responsibility of managing the world's largest public collection of dolls. Out of the 20,000 dolls at Strong Museum, 12,000 are three-dimensional dolls and 8,000 are paper dolls. The museum actively acquires more dolls every year, so the collection continues to grow.

Many of the dolls in Strong Museum's collection can be found in exhibitions such as *When Barbie Dated G.I. Joe: America's Romance with Cold War Toys, Betty Boop to Barney: Make-Believe Characters Invade the Marketplace* and *Between Two Worlds: African-American Identity in American Culture.* In these exhibits, dolls reflect certain American cultural values, such as those relating to gender roles, consumerism, and identity.

On the museum's second floor, 5,000 dolls are on permanent display within study cases. Here doll connoisseur and novice alike can feast their eyes on the immense variety of dolls that come from countries all over the world, and which are made from every type of material imaginable. If that's not enough, there are also rotating displays of dolls. Here one can get a close-up view of certain dolls, most of which are on public display for the first time, such as the paper dolls. These displays, which explore themes such as patriotism, bride dolls, and famous personalities, change annually.

With this publication, Strong Museum's educational mission extends beyond the boundaries of the museum's walls. When you open this book, you can view Strong Museum dolls in the comfort of your own home. Think of it as a portable museum exhibit that one can take anywhere. It is just another way in which the Strong Museum is reaching out to those who want to learn about dolls and American culture.

Here in this book, one can see many of the strengths of Strong Museum's collection. For example, the museum has one of the most definitive collections of Martha Chase dolls. It includes a very rare set of "Alice in Wonderland" characters, and many of the original manufacturer's molds for these dolls.

Other highlights include the quantity of Izannah Walker and Ludwig Greiner dolls at Strong Museum. With so many of these dolls available for study, it can become a connoisseur's dream to compare and contrast the subtle variations among these dolls. The same would hold true for the printed cloth dolls, both cut and uncut, that are in the museum's collection.

Overall, you can view this book as just "the tip of the iceberg." We hope that it will tantalize you enough to think about visiting the museum, located in Rochester, New York. For more information call 716-263-2700. Enjoy this publication from Strong Museum, where exploring American Life is serious fun!

Strong Museum, Rochester, New York.

On the museum's second floor, 5,000 dolls are on display within study cases.

AUTHOR'S NOTE

When I began this adventure through Strong Museum's vast collections of dolls to select those which best represent America's contribution to the world of dolls, I thought anew about the extent to which the humble doll mirrors life. In the early months of this venture I was almost a tenant at Strong Museum, studying their dolls, organizing my selections and composing the photo layouts by materials and messages inherent in their designs. During this time, I came to know the museum in its broader scope. It is a compelling museum which explores American life, often poignantly through its special exhibits. In them, dolls were present in one way or another, as ephemeral reflections of society, its costumes or customs, or as retrospective miniature representations of important historical figures or events which shaped our country. It was exciting to consider the reach of dolls throughout American life.

The commercial manufacture of dolls in America does not begin until the 19th century, but the importance of dolls, homemade or imported, in American childhood has much deeper roots. Although the main focus of this book is American-made dolls, studied by the material of which they are made, a few significant "immigrant" dolls from the early centuries are included in the overview, for they too, within their context, are part of the broader story. Changing times and changing attitudes toward chidren are reflected in dolls and doll play. Dolls as playthings stimulate imagination. They are nurtured by children who express compassion or gain companionship through these early relationships. Just as children teach their dolls, dolls teach us of their young owners and of their time and place. Dolls are viewed by many as little pieces of history and art, and as such also deserve our respect and consideration. In understanding or assessing their intrinsic value and how they fit into their time, a consideration of what was happening when they were made and played with expands an appreciation of these beloved but often "used up" objects. While events can often only suggest what may have been, they point to the factors that influenced the American people in making dolls that spoke to them then and speak to us now.

As my involvement with the subject grew, I found myself writing this book with love, with love for dolls, for the generations of American children who have played with them, for the spirit of the people who made them — the mothers, fathers and businessmen and women — for fellow doll collectors who cherish the wider significance of dolls as elements of art and history, with love for my country that these dolls reflect and with a love for the power of words — and sometimes humor — to convey all that and more. I hope you will share my feelings in this celebration of the American doll.

— Dorothy McGonagle

HISTORICAL PERSPECTIVE

A DISTANT VIEW

The study of American dolls is a multifaceted endeavor. It reveals many aspects of the social and cultural history of our country as well as the countries of our ancestors. Playthings in general, and dolls very specifically, mirror the moment in which they are created. They speak to us of what their designers or makers considered important. At the same time they reflect technological developments, political statements, personal ingenuity, whimsey, and perhaps most of all, love. Education and entertainment co-exist in the nursery, by design or default. Thus the dolls which have survived over the last three centuries give us a picture of American life, values, hopes, and certainly of American pride.

The primary considerations in this book are the dolls that were actually made in America and made for play. In the subsequent sections, they are grouped by the type of material of which they are made, or more specifically of which the head is made. We generally think of a doll as a child's plaything, and indeed dolls have existed as long as there have been children. However, through the ages, various civilizations have used dolls for many purposes beyond play, and so a brief look at that history is perhaps a proper beginning place.

Ancient civilizations made dolls, and undoubtedly those children played with dolls. Their primary purpose, however, had been for adults who believed these miniature representations of people had religious or magical powers. These figures include ancestral images, idols, fetishes, and talismans, which were ascribed various powers ranging from protection to vengeance or fertility. A detailed examination of these ancient variants can be found in Max von Boehn's 1932 work, *Dolls and Puppets*. In brief, ancestor images represent the dead who remain present in spirit. During the ceremonial process of remembering the departed and attempting to gain intervention and protection from the unseen other world, the image, anointed with holy oils or otherwise revered, becomes an idol, itself venerated.

The dolls found in ancient graves were likely not beloved toys but representations of humans, placed with departed persons to accompany them on their journey to the unknown. The Egyptian paddle doll, dating from 2000 B.C., has a wooden body shaped like a boat paddle and strings of clay beads for hair. It was long thought to have been a charming child's toy. Archaeologists, however, have found numerous such "dolls" in the graves of princes; it is now believed they represent concubines for the departed. Having no legs, they cannot run away...not exactly the plaything we might sentimentalize. However, other sources such as drawings and writings do acknowledge ancient dolls as playthings. In ancient Greece, as von Boehn notes, girls played with dolls until marriage, when they left their dolls at the temple of Artemis — a symbol of leaving childhood

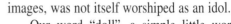

Illustration 1. Rainbow Hummingbird Kachina (80.4645), cottonwood, Hopi ca 1950.

behind. The Bible (1 Corinthians 13: 11) records a more forthright act: "Now that I have become a man, I have put away the things of a child." Twentieth century doll collectors know this is no longer necessary.

To the best of our knowledge, some of the first dolls made on the American continent were the Kachina dolls of the Pueblo Indians which were carved of cactus root or soft woods, like cottonwood or pine, brightly painted and adorned with feathers [*Illustration 1*]. They had deep religious significance, each representing a spirit or kachina which was invoked during ceremonial rites. After this use, however, the kachina dolls were given to the children to teach them the important aspects of their religion. Education through entertainment was made possible because the kachina doll, unlike earlier images, was not itself worshiped as an idol.

Our word "doll"...a simple little word with many meanings...is worth consideration. It first appears in the early 1700s and is thought by some to be rooted in the word "idol" which seems to be a heavy burden for a plaything. The English had long used the words "poppet" and "baby" to represent the child's toy; the *Encyclopedia Britannica* records that in 1759 George Washington ordered from his London agent an assortment of books for children just beginning to read and a "fashionable dressed baby to cost 10 shillings". Both the French and the German words for doll (poupeé and puppe) are, like our puppet, derived from the Latin, "pupa", defined as a baby not yet named. Earlier Germans also used the word "docke" (meaning little block of wood, precisely the material used) for doll, and in Germanic countries today that term is still used. Dictionaries through the ages have defined "doll" in various ways. With so many types of dolls having been made over the years, we constantly need to modify the word: play doll, baby doll, artist doll, reproduction doll. It's a lot of work for this one little word "doll" to do. I am reminded of the great expert on utterance, Humpty Dumpty, who told Alice "when I use a word, it means just what I choose it to mean, neither more nor less...when I make a word do a lot of work, I always pay it extra." "Doll" would have done well on his payroll.

The commercial manufacture of dolls in 19th and 20th century America provides a great deal of information on the history of the play doll, but a consideration of what has gone before enhances our understanding. First and foremost, it is necessary to remember that most of our peoples emigrated here from Europe in our early years, and so, too, did our dolls. In recent years, our doll production reflects the diverse ancestral persuasions and historical figures which seasoned the character of our immense country.

While information on European dolls produced in the Middle Ages is only slowly coming to light, a frequently reproduced 1491 illustration from the German publication *Hortus Sanitatis*, provides documentation on dollmaking as an industry in Nuremberg. The dollmaker is shown fashioning clay dolls and several of these types survive in the Germanisches National Museum in Nuremberg. Most of these have a circular depression in the chest, which may have held a coin for religious purposes. Although they may have been used as Christian baptismal gifts, it is also a reasonable assumption they afterwards served as toys.

The First European Dolls in America. Less than a century after Columbus' travels, in 1585, we find a record of the first European dolls in America. One of the members of the Roanoke expedition, sponsored by Sir Walter Raleigh, was John White. Fortunately for America's documented history, White was a fine artist whose drawings of the events included a Native American "Indian wyfe" and her little girl who is holding a doll dressed in Elizabethan costume [*Illustration 2*]. Presumably this was a gift by a member of the Roanoke party and it is apparent that the child is delighted with the toy.

English author Antonia Fraser in *A History of Toys* aptly refers to the gifts, including dolls, given to these Native Americans as "weapons of friendship". University of Rochester historian Ian Gordon in his paper entitled *Children, Play and Dolls in America 1880-1940* addressed the symbolism inherent in this Elizabethan doll. Signifying "English culture and power" for both the English and Native Americans and "meant to inspire awe and respect for the invading "civilized culture", the doll, Gordon states, was clearly not a plaything. For the adults, this may well have been the case; however, the young child in White's drawing appears to feel otherwise. It is possible that once back in their home, the child was not allowed to play with the doll, which would reinforce the symbolism noted. An article in *Doll Reader®*, May 1987 by America's noted doll researchers Dorothy S. and Evelyn Jane Coleman shows this drawing [*Illustration 3*] along with a 1590 engraving made by Theodor de Bry in England which was published the same year in a volume called *America*. It is copied from the White drawing, but with distinctly English overtones. The doll's costume has much more Elizabethan detail and the child is portrayed with one hand over her head waving, flag-like, a classic English rattle, more illustrative of the symbolism which Gordon notes. The features of the mother and child in the de Bry engraving are also much more European, perhaps intentionally, but the expression of delight on the child's face in John White's drawing was definitely lost in the translation. While the comparison is significant, it is the particularly powerful White drawing which clearly illustrates the recorded word "They are greatly Delighted with puppets and babes which wear brought out of England."

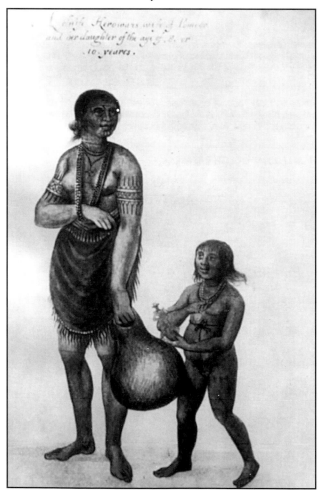

Illustration 2. Drawing by John White, member of the Roanoke expedition, 1585. Handwritten in ink at the top are the words: "A chiefe Herowars wyfe of Pomeoc and her daughter of the age of .8 or .10 years." *Courtesy of the Smithsonian Institution, photograph no. 18725.*

Illustration 3. Engraving by Theodor de Bry based on the John White drawing, published in England in 1590. Note the addition of a rattle and the more elaborate costume on the doll. *Courtesy of the Smithsonian Institution, photograph no. 57527.*

17ᵀᴴ CENTURY
EARLY COLONIAL SETTLEMENTS

In 1607 Jamestown, Virginia became the first permanent English settlement. While there is no doubt that some dolls were brought to this country or made by parents during the first century of settlement, few childhood trinkets and tales exist today. Survival itself was the aim of the various expeditions that colonized our shores. Nearly half the children born in this period did not reach the age of five years, and considering the struggle survival entailed, it was expedient for them to take on adult responsibility as quickly as possible. Additionally, since older children shared in the care of their younger siblings, the doll as a plaything might have been considered somewhat superfluous.

The business of building a new life was paramount and encompassed the need for shelter, food, government, education, and religion. It is also important to remember that in our earliest years the social structure of the colonies consisted primarily of the wealthy governing minority and the vast majority of poorer, simple, hard-working peoples striving to make a better life for themselves and their future generations. Although recreation and childhood play were not priorities for the majority, those who prospered enjoyed some imported luxuries and their children probably knew commercial toys.

Childhood in early America. The average 17th century American child was not a pampered pet (that pleasured state was still at least two centuries away) but instead played with simple toys such as balls, marbles, tops, kites, and dolls, all basically homemade items. While children have a natural instinct to play and much learning is accomplished even in tempered frolic, learning was the primary goal for children. Even when not directly religious, teaching still had religious overtones and undercurrents, as in John Cotton's 1646 *Spiritual Milk Drawn out of the Breasts of Both Testaments, Chiefly for the Spiritual Nourishment of Boston Babes in either England* which is believed to have been the first book for children printed in British colonial America. Fortunately "Sunday toys" such as the Noah's Ark were also acceptable and allowed for some imaginative play.

In a well-researched publication from the Strong Museum, *A Century of Childhood 1820-1920*, Karin Calvert notes: "The ability to stand was the most visible of uniquely human characteristics, and it is significant in Western culture that the word 'upright' came to refer to both physical and moral stature. Nearly all of the artifacts designed for children before 1770 existed to make the child upright." Swaddling and stays imposed a prematurely dignified demeanor, walking stools held the child vertical, and prevented the dreadful and animalistic baseness of crawling; simultaneously, the moral fiber of the child's being was molded as he or she was launched into adult behavior and responsibilities.

Other types of informal education continued at home with a focus on gender-specific behaviorial training. Boys trained for a variety of activities — marksmanship, shooting bows and arrows, hunting and fishing. In contrast, girls focused their efforts on learning and perfecting needlework and other textile related skills.

The following excerpt from Katharine Morrison McClinton's *Antiques of American Childhood* details the astonishing array of decorative needle skills taught an aspiring young colonial girl:

"Dresden on Lawn and Muslin, and Work in Imitation of Brussells Lace...Shell-Work, and Flowers for the Head," samplers, "Embroidery in Gold and Silver, and all Sorts of shaded work in Colours," filigree, "Turkey-work", flourishing, "Brocaded-Work for Handkerchiefs," "Silk Embroidery's of every kind, Tambour, Feather, India and Darning, Spriggings, with a Variety of Open-work to each; Tapestry, plain lined and drawn Cat-gut black and white, with a Number of beautiful Stitches, Diaper and plain Darnings, French-quilting, Knitting, various sorts of Marking with the Embellishments of Royal-cross, Plain-cross, Queen, Irish and Ten Stitches, Plain-work and Baby-linnen of the newest Taste."

Equally remarkable is the tender age at which these skills were learned. Skillfully executed samplers completed by girls well under the age of ten attest to the many hours spent in this diligent manner. One can assume that an occasional doll was born from, or benefitted by, these talents, but such frivolity was not the primary purpose behind this industrious effort.

Art of the period records dolls in aristocratic family portraiture; it is likely some of the wealthy families brought dolls, which no longer exist, to America. These settlers also carried with them rich 17th century Northern European traditions including a love of dolls' houses, which was very much an adult fancy. Dollhouses may have been created here at that time, even though the earliest surviving American-made doll or baby house was found in the Van Cortlandt Mansion in New York, and dates a century later, 1744. It reflects Dutch traditions, illustrates Dutch influenced colonial architecture, as well as provides insight into the type of play that more privileged 17th century children were permitted. The building of a dolls' house acknowledges an interaction between parents and children that other, more ephemeral, toys and dolls cannot.

The Native Americans of the Northeast had taught the early settlers how to grow and use corn, first for food, then for the cornhusk doll, ephemeral creations which have not survived. Other types of dolls that do not survive from this period are simple little homemade rag dolls that a mother would have fashioned or the equally simple wooden doll whittled by a father's hand. These were the plain, homely (in all the best senses of the word) treasures of a child, the representations of a parent's love. Despite the disdain of idleness preached in America, the occasional use of a diversionary tactic or toy was surely employed and likely enjoyed, and probably not just by the child. Sadly, with the mortality rate so high, we can surmise that some cloth dolls or other trinkets made to comfort sick children accompanied them to the grave, even though this practice was frowned upon by Christian churches. Others might have been cast away by future generations who found them cruder than those which could then be obtained as more toys were imported into the New World.

Meanwhile in Germany, a 1665 engraving, entitled Kinder-spel or Children's Games, records children at play with a great variety of toys and games [*Illustration 4*]. Children carrying fifes and drums are marching in a band, some boys are flying kites, walking on stilts, performing acrobatics, playing with jumpropes, tops and windmill toys. Boys and girls are engaged in a lively game of blind man's buff, while in the foreground, two little girls are playing with their dolls, surrounded by an array of miniature household paraphernalia. It is a joyful and almost timeless scene, depicting the universal nature of the playthings and documenting that the German toy industry was indeed flourishing at this time. The German emigres to this country brought with them this rich heritage; in the later 18th and 19th centuries the American child would be more in a position to partake of this bounty.

Illustration 4. A 1665 engraving entitled Kinder-spel records children at play with a great variety of toys and games. Kinderspel is from A. Fraser's *A History of Toys*.

18TH CENTURY
IMMIGRANT ENGLISH WOODEN DOLLS, FOR PLAY OR TO SHOW FASHION

At the opening of the 18th century, the settler population of the colonies was approximately 275,000 (*Academic American Encyclopedia*). The doll population remained unrecorded, but in January 1902 the *Ladies Home Journal* heralded a story of a doll then over 200 years old named Letitia Penn. Indeed, Letitia had that most treasured certification, a written provenance. Attached to the 1865 will of a Mary B. Kirk was a note attesting that the doll was brought from England in 1699 by William Penn as a gift from his daughter, Letitia, to a little girl in Philadelphia. The note further listed the chain of caring owners in the Quaker community through whose hands Letitia passed until being given to Mary Kirk some seven years earlier. This was a recorded lineage unparalleled in American doll history. Unfortunately, four score and some years later, doll historians on both sides of the Atlantic concurred that Letitia most likely dates not to her reputed 1699 arrival in America as a trusted traveling companion of William Penn en route to settle Pennsylvania, but rather to the period of 1720-1740. The story is well recounted by Ann Bahar in the April 1989 *Doll Reader*®. The doll known as Letitia Penn now resides in the Historical Society of Pennsylvania, whose administrators were responsible for the efforts to verify her history. These answers have raised other questions: was there an even earlier doll that traveled with William Penn, or could Letitia have arrived with William Penn's son Thomas, when he came to take over management of his father's colony? That time frame, 1720-40, is consistent with what appears to be Letitia's own. It is easy to understand how a story and its dates can become muddled in only one generation: my three children, when all in their twenties, all lay claim to one bedraggled stuffed dog, and even I, dog purchaser, am not sure which of the older two is right.

According to Bahar's research, Letitia Penn's dress was made from bits of narrow strips of cloth stitched together, so typical of her era when fabric was hand loomed, extremely expensive, and not to be wasted on a doll. She had probably been purchased unclothed and dressed at home from "the memories of dozens of dresses". Letitia was, though, an imported and important play doll, and as such, demonstrates changes in the attitudes toward children during the 18th century.

In historical societies and museums, particularly those of Northeastern America, there are other such English wooden babies. Some of these dolls were initially imported to show the newest fashions. When a model wearing the latest style arrived, a fortunate family or child often acquired the older one, but it may have been maintained as a doll for show or for admiration rather than for play. While the "wax baby" which George Washington ordered in 1759 does not survive, some of these early dolls were dearly treasured within their initial families and passed along from generation to generation. Some still retain their original given or child owner's name, thus attaining historical significance commensurate with their appeal. Mary Jenkins, a documented 1745 emigre to New York, is on proud

display at the Museum of the City of New York. Polly Sumner, a 1776 Boston lady, has retired to the Boston State House. The Peabody-Essex Museum in Salem, Massachusetts also houses a number of original family dolls from the 18th century, some of which have been redressed as they were passed down to later generations. One Queen Anne wooden doll is particularly noteworthy; she was repainted black and given a curly black wig to represent an African American, probably in the mid-19th century. Today she silently speaks volumes.

The unnamed but magnificent wooden doll from the Strong Museum, seen in *illustration 5,* carries no provenance to be cherished or refuted, so she, too, speaks silently of her past. She is English, like her counterparts dating from the first half of the 18th century and the product of either an itinerant or home-bound craftsman rather than a factory. Wood turners by trade often turned to dollmaking and once skilled, individual styles developed. The basic form of the English wooden doll underwent change slowly, which makes precise dating quite difficult. Additionally, as noted by doll historian Maurine S. Popp, the trend toward simplification in the carving of wooden dolls throughout the 18th century is probably only one part of their evolution. Maurine suggests there were less detailed versions being made concurrent with the more elaborate examples, priced more cheaply to appeal to thinner pocketbooks. This premise would of course complicate dating any of these dolls, and might alter the birthdate of Letitia herself. Only an occasional American colonial child was fortunate enough to own a doll like this.

Growth of the Colonies. The 18th century saw dramatic growth in the American population as well as an increase in trade and manufacturing. Settlers like the German Jews, being primarily merchants and traders, continued to bring a heritage rich in toymaking to our shores. While the German toy manufacturing centers were well established, colonial trade at this time was greatest with England. However, the roots were being planted for the future. But many children throughout the colonies continued to keep company only with homemade dolls.

Other dolls were made by Native American tribes both for their own use as well as for trade, which documented their diverse tribal costumes. Some of the tribes used glass beads and quillwork as a form of decoration. Because these dolls were exotic souvenirs, they were often protected by the adults.

During the Revolutionary war, anti-English sentiment was high and British products were scorned, leaving the door open for imports from other countries, especially Germany.

Many early communities have been rebuilt and are maintained as living history museums. Plimoth Plantation and Sturbridge Village in Massachusetts and Colonial Williamsburg in Virginia are notable among those places where families can actively take part in reliving and understanding the past. A similar interest in compre-

Illustration 5. English wooden doll (75.3093), first half of the 18th century. Head is gesso covered and painted, glass eyes, all wood turned body, original clothes, 21-1/2 inches (54.6 cm) tall.

Felicity. Education is reinforced as today's child plays out the stories of time past with her doll. A long standing concept of 19th and 20th century doll manufacturers to dress dolls in historical costume was epitomized in the exquisitely rendered 1939 Effanbee Historical Series noted in *illustration 6*. These efforts combine play and learning in an interactive and engaging way.

The Post-Revolutionary Period. In 1787 the Founding Fathers drew up the Constitution and in 1789 George Washington became the first president of the United States of America. Hero, soldier, statesman, and family man, the patriot Washington would become a venerable subject for doll makers, mothers and fathers, from his time forward. The following year the U.S. Patent Office was opened, but it would be nearly 70 years before a Philadelphia man, Ludwig Greiner, would register the first American doll patent. Philadelphia, the nation's birthplace and capital until 1800, would see the establishment of many doll makers and distributors over the next two centuries.

During this period Salem, Massachusetts had become the principal American port for the China trade, a route which helped America recover from the crippling effects of the British blockade during the Revolution. Many a sea captain also brought European dolls to this country through Salem, a provenance given to too many dolls from that town over the years. By now, most of these dolls have found their way into collections or historical societies, but hopefully others still remain in their original homes, forgotten in the attic or cherished in safekeeping.

hending history and educating children through play is seen in the current American Girls collection of dolls, books, and accessories from the Pleasant Company. Various periods in America's past are represented by different dolls, with each era thoroughly researched for historical accuracy at national resource centers including Colonial Williamsburg and the Strong Museum. A colonial girl whose story is set in Williamsburg in 1774 is depicted by the doll, Trade with other European countries had been stepped up, and soon the toys and dolls of Germany and Holland were being brought in increasing numbers to the more urban American child. By the early 19th century stylish little German peg wooden dolls (of the type shown in *Illustration 7*) were taking their place alongside the still more prevalent homemade rag dolls in the homes and hearts of America's young.

Illustration 6. Effanbee Historical Series display doll and "replica" as sold in 1939. Representing the year 1760, these are the cover dolls of the book *The Elegance of Effanbee* by Nancy F. Carlson, which details the entire series of 30 dolls. *Photo courtesy Dave Carlson.*

Illustration 7.
German peg
wooden doll, ca.
1810. *Maurine S.
Popp Collection.*

EARLY 19TH CENTURY
EXPANSION, SELF-SUFFICIENCY AND HOMEMADE DOLLS

By the onset of the 19th century, the country had nearly doubled in size and the U.S. census recorded over five million inhabitants. In 1812, Congress declared war against Great Britain and sporadic land and sea battles erupted over the next two years. Declared blockades damaged our economy, both in the private sector and for the federal government whose major source of revenue was from duties on imports. Kindled by this inability to receive goods from abroad, American manufacturing increased dramatically. The minimal importation coupled with the effort expended on producing goods previously imported postponed the onset of an American doll industry and helps explain the sparse number of European dolls which exist from this era.

During the War of 1812 the term "Uncle Sam" was first coined to personify the federal government. While it is not known just when the first Uncle Sam doll was made, it was probably an individual effort, representing a political statement. However, Uncle Sam subsequently became a consistent character in commercial American dollmaking and was even produced later in Germany, in recognition of America and American personalities. Several examples in *illustration 8* show how he came to be represented over time.

Handmade Dolls. Trade and strife with the Native Americans continued; among the survivors are the extraordinary pair of dolls in *illustration 9*, from the Rosalie Whyel Museum of Doll Art in Bellevue, Washington. Without a known history, these English wooden dolls may simply have been twice traded, first as unclothed doll-babies perhaps for furs, then dressed by the Cree Indians in tribal costume for special presentation. They are quite remarkable and simply wonderful, but, oh, if only they could tell the tales of where they've been and what they've seen.

The spirit of the pioneers and their apparent zest for life seems to indicate that play, including doll play, would have been readily accommodated. Dolls that could not make the trip in a crowded wagon were likely replaced as soon as possible.

Pride, self-confidence and optimism defined the young nation. Art and literature increasingly celebrated the American experience, while architecture and design began to show a more identifiable American style. The homegrown dolls of this period are truly the dolls of the American people. They were often humble creations of cloth and wood or other natural materials that were at hand, such as nuts, leather, bone, and twigs. Several examples are seen in the wood and cloth sections of this book, in addition to the handsome large lady in *illustration 10*. Usually called folk or primitive dolls because their makers were unschooled in the arts, it can be argued

Illustration 8. A variety of Uncle Sams include a Palmer Cox Brownie ninepin (74.1487) by McLoughlin Bros., ca 1892, 12in (30cm) and a deeply modeled bisque headed Uncle Sam (76.1851) ca. 1895, 16in (41cm) standing in front of a wooden bond salesman display board (76.4583), ca 1915.

Illustration 9. Pair of English wooden babies, a 16in (41cm) man, a 13in (33cm) woman and a 7-1/4in (18cm) replacement wax-over composition baby in marvelous cradleboard, dressed by the Cree Indians of the Northeastern American continent, ca 1790-1820, exhibiting elaborate bead and quillwork. As in America, these native Canadian Cree peoples were affected by trade with Europeans. A study by Susan Hedrick, Curator, Rosalie Whyel Museum of Doll Art, in the Jan/Feb 1997 *Antique Doll World* details these dolls and a similar pair in their time frame as reflections of a culture's history. *Photo courtesy Rosalie Whyel Museum of Doll Art.*

they had the greatest training of all, a knowledge of or love for the recipient. Wendy Lavitt, in her book entitled *American Folk Dolls*, records numerous 19th century adult women's vibrant memories of cherished dolls. One, named Polly, was a rag doll belonging to a Quaker child in the first decade of the 19th century. This doll endured numerous cosmetic surgeries and limb replacements. She lost her head to a plaster replacement, and then to others through the years. She, or should I say "they", were well-remembered. Occasionally one of these cloth doll creations received several new cloth faces throughout its lifetime, each attached over the previous faded or soiled one. It is always a thrill to discover one a century or more later. All of these handmade dolls tell a story without words and each is a reflection of its time and circumstances such as the handmade wooden lady in *illustration 11*.

Childhood: A distinct and special time. Several autobiographies by 19th century women, including Lucy Larcom's *A New England Girlhood* and Caroline A. Stickney's *A Daughter of the Puritans* mention doll play along with spirited tree-climbing and sledding. Larcom refers to "numerous rag-children" and Stickney relates a baptism of a doll performed at age seven, which she recalled as an "unpardonable sin against the Holy Ghost." Their vivid recollections paint a bright picture of childhood, but their freedom, however, ended abruptly with adolescence and the entrance into womanhood and all its conventions. So many different women tell the same story, and yet, even when fettered by adult requirements the spirit born of their childhood liberty drove these women through their lives. By mid-century, the passionate sorrow at childhood lost was voiced in the writings of women including Louisa May Alcott in her time-honored novel *Little Women*. These three

Illustration 10. Large primitive cloth lady (79.9981) with carefully hand-painted features. This rosy-cheeked, blue-eyed, raven-haired serene presence is nearly as big as life at 29in (73.5cm). From around 1895.

Illustration 11. Happy primitive 14in (35.5cm) carved wooden and painted lady (75.518) from the second half of the 19th century has hinged joints to allow her to dance or jump. The word "Wrigley" written on her back remains a tantalizing clue to her origins.

noted 19th century books are discussed by Anne Scott MacLeod in *A Century of Childhood* in which she carefully addresses American girlhood. G. Stanley Hall's 1897 *A Study of Dolls* and other references to doll play (up through age fifteen) further acknowledges 19th century childhood, particularly for girls, as being as prolonged as possible. This stands in sharp contrast to the child of today racing towards the perceived freedoms of adult life.

MID 19TH CENTURY
INGENUITY, INDUSTRIALIZATION, A BUDDING AMERICAN DOLL INDUSTRY

Industrialization created a growing middle class; its business and professional men could afford the new manufactured items, which became symbols of their success. While dolls were a part of this new consumerism, the vast majority of manufactured dolls, made of wood, papier-mâché, wax or china, were still imported into this country from England, France and Germany. However, an American industry was beginning to emerge. Of singular importance was Charles Goodyear's accidental discovery of a process of stabilizing rubber at a high temperature — called vulcanization — which he patented in 1844. Seven years later, Goodyear exhibited numerous rubber articles in London and in his 1855 autobiography *Gum Elastic and Its Varieties*, he listed one thousand articles, including "dolls, toys and trifles" made of this material. Many of these heads were formed in molds taken from German porcelain or papier-mâché dolls — a technique employed by other early American manufacturers using other materials. The 1869 H.G.Norton wholesale rubber goods catalog shows several such examples copied in this way. Because he was deeply in debt, Goodyear licensed his patent quite cheaply, and never realized the financial benefits his discovery warranted. Also, because his patent was for a process of making a viable material, and did not specifically mention a doll, it is not considered the first American doll patent. It will also be seen that other manufacturing companies turned to dolls as a sideline in answer to a growing interest in the production of playthings.

Ludwig Greiner of Philadelphia was awarded the first American doll patent in 1858. Greiner was a German emigre who had been in the doll business in his homeland and patented a papier-mâché or composition doll head reinforced with fabric at the seams and in the nose. Virtually indistinguishable from the imported German products prevalent at the time, Greiner's doll heads heralded a new American commerce.

The initial stirrings of commercially manufactured American dolls had begun in cottage industries in various locations, with the dollmaker-proprietor providing products for the immediate local area. Izannah Walker of Central Falls, Rhode Island, began this way, probably as early as the late 1840s, making cloth dolls with molded features, painted in the sophisticated "primitive" style of noted portrait artists of the mid-century. *Illustration 12* shows a classic example of the first cloth doll patented in America in 1873. Several other Izannah Walker dolls are shown in the cloth section of this book, pages 90-91; collectively they reveal the diversity and similarity in one artist's work.

Other related technological advancements include the sewing machine and photography. The sewing machine represented a pivotal breakthrough in technology. Although first patented in 1846 by Elias Howe, it is, however, the name of Isaac Merrit Singer that became synonymous with this new product. Singer, of Oswego, New York worked as a mechanic from the age of twelve. He became intrigued with sewing machines while repairing a primitive version, and patented his improvements in 1851. Singer had great business sense and, recognizing the value of advertising, was soon the leader in the field. Patenting 20 improvements over the years, Singer brought his product into the homes of America, altering domestic sewing and facilitating individual and cottage industry dollmaking. Looking into the attachment drawer of a century-old Singer, one sees an amazing array of twisted metal tuckers, pleaters, rufflers, quilters and underbraiders — the elaborate hand-stitchery of yore incarnated and fossilized.

The evolution of photography as a technical advancement and as an art form allowed events to be recorded visually and instantly. Photography enabled people to see everything from the wild west to contemporary heroes and their families. This documentation changed the face of recorded history and conveniently paralleled the time frame of the development of the American doll industry. Occasionally photographs included children playing with their dolls or those which a studio photographer main-

Illustration 12. Tranquil Izannah Walker cloth doll (73.1478) 18in (45.5cm), patented in 1873, has oil painted features and classic hairstyle with two long curls in front of ears. One can readily imagine a child hanging her prized bell on her treasured doll.

tained as props. Photos record Native American children with imported German dolls which beg for more information, while others show children playing with miniature tepees and cradleboards, a mixture of cultures following no strict rules. Probably the finest and most complete photographic record of one American town is found in the books compiled by Dr. Thomas A. and Joan W. Gandy, from the nearly century-long collection of photographs taken by Norman's Studio of Natchez, Mississippi. Their *Natchez Victorian Children, 1865-1915* is a visual delight in which the decades roll by, showing subtle changes in the beautiful children sensitively photographed and the local events, many of them charity benefits, which have been forever documented. French fashion dolls and German bisque girl dolls take their places with their owners, but no American-made examples were found in the published photographs. The dolls brought to the studio were probably considered the "best"; but surely at home, homemade cloth or other American dolls lived alongside these in the nursery. Old photographs provide a spectrum of valuable information, sometimes confirming that one picture is worth a thousand words.

Many Americans came to see the newest inventions and latest products at huge fairs or expositions, patterned after those which had met with great success in Europe. The 1853 New York Crystal Palace exposition included an exhibit of dolls by importer George W. Tuttle of New York. The exhibit was illustrated in Gleason's 1853 *Pictorial Drawing-Room Companion* and is reproduced on page 92 of the Coleman *Collector's Book of Dolls Clothes*. These dolls were described as surpassing "anything we have ever seen, both in tasteful design, and beauty of decoration", and earned Tuttle an Honorable Mention. At the other end of the spectrum were the inexpensive little solid china dolls called bathing dolls or "Frozen Charlottes" which were imported in great quantities from mid-century onward. The name Frozen Charlotte was inspired by a popular New England ballad of the 1860s which tells the tale of a young girl who set out in an open sleigh with her beau one winter night for a ball some fifteen miles away. Despite the exceptionally cold weather, she refused to wrap herself in blankets, for she wanted to be seen in her silken cloak. When they arrived, she was frozen, dead, having paid the dearest price for her vanity.

Travel journals also shed light on the variety of dolls that peopled a child's world. In *The Journal of Mary Chipman Lawrence on the Whaler Addison 1856-1860*, the author describes the treasured playthings of her six year old daughter, Minnie:

September 27, 1857
"For the last week I have been making a doll and dressing it for her to carry in port, as Sarah Price [Minnie's other doll] seems to have seen her best days. She calls this one Mary Stuart.

March 28, 1858
"Minnie met with about as severe an affliction as she ever experienced today. She lost her Frankie overboard, a doll that she dearly loved for its own sake and the more because it was Grandma Anne's. She cried for a long time and wrung her hands in the greatest agony. She insisted so much upon have black clothes made to wear, that I was obliged to get a piece of black ribbon to tie on her arm to pacify her."

Aside from Sarah Price, Mary Stuart and Frankie, Minnie also had a small china doll named Emma Shepard. She took what appears to be a doll-like figure she christened Billy Buttons to bed and couldn't go to sleep without him.

The above entries indicate that Minnie personalized her dolls with both a first and last name and owned both female and male companions for different purposes. Some were played with, others were slept with; they could also be homemade, heirloom or store bought.

The Civil War Period. Histories and haunting stories abound, during this time, including some touching tales involving dolls. One recounted by Alice Kent Trimpey in *Becky...My First Love* tells of a lad of fifteen who in 1861 had left with a Wisconsin regiment when it was "called to the colors." After the last goodbyes, his young sweetheart made her way to him and slipped her dearest keepsake, her own tiny doll, into his hand. He died in battle, was later buried in Arlington Cemetery, and when his personal things were sent home, the box held only his jacket with the doll still in the pocket, where he had carried it

Illustration 14. This English wax over composition (76.887), 18-1/2in (47cm), ca 1850 lady may have been costumed for the London World's Fair of 1851 or for a Sanitary Fair benefit. She has wire-operated sleeping glass eyes and a slit in her head for a wig. A patriotic striped apron bears thirteen stars on the bodice, but the rosettes at her ears are the tour de force!

Illustration 13. Drawing of Sanitary Fair doll used in Horsman Doll Company brochure, ca 1955.

German-made lady with blonde molded hair was probably sold as a head only and made up into a pincushion with grand patriotic fashion by her owner [*Illustration 15*]. The Ives mechanical toy shown as the frontispiece of this book also celebrates the women of the war, the Daughters of the Regiment, an honorary title given those women whose parents served.

Alaska: The next frontier. The purchase of Alaska in 1867 opened up yet another new arena for adventure, real or invented. When people began settling there, it brought the Alaskan natives, the Eskimo or Inuit people, the Aleuts, and the Alaskan Indian tribes into the American vernacular. These native Americans have a rich history of dollmaking using their indigenous materials, [*Illustration 16*], to make play dolls for their children and in later years, dolls for export and trade as souvenirs. Doll making provided lessons in producing and decorating clothing using the same materials incorporated in human clothing for children and adults. By the early 20th century, clothing for humans and for dolls might include materials which reflected early native traditions, such as seal fur and intestine, feathers and animal leather, wool and cotton fabric, glass beads, and animal hair.

Recreation and Leisure. Through the 19th century, an increased emphasis was placed on leisure and sport. Horse racing, popular since colonial times, continued to hold the interest of

for three years, his constant companion and a reminder of one who loved him. Another German parian doll, in a private Massachusetts collection, wrapped in a child's plaid shawl, still today has a note pinned to her dress with the owner's name and the notation that as a little girl she had worn the shawl and carried the doll to see the Union boys come marching home. The significance of this event, the memory of the doll as an active participant, and the recorded note, all tell us a great deal about the importance some dolls held for their owners.

Women of both the North and South served as nurses at the front and in hospitals. At home they held benefits called "Sanitary Fairs" to raise money for medical supplies for the Sanitary Commission, the forerunner of the Red Cross. Women's magazines printed patterns for dressing dolls in patriotic or regimental costume which were then sold or raffled for the cause. These dolls were given prominent spots in homes; one survivor currently in a private collection in Massachusetts has a documented history of having been in the window of her Boston area home throughout the war. A drawing of this Sanitary Fair doll, *illustration 13*, was used a century later by the Horsman Doll Company in a brochure. Two other dolls dressed with patriotic flair, perhaps for Sanitary Fairs, are seen here. The English wax-over composition example is finely dressed, in a commercial manner, probably during the pre-war years [*Illustration 14*]. The

Americans, while the more family-oriented traveling circus, notably P.T. Barnum's "Greatest Show on Earth", gained popularity. Baseball was fast becoming the national pastime. Ice skating and roller skating, lawn tennis, cycling, seaside bathing and slow swimming were popular for adults and children, and these led to fashions designed for each particular sport. Versions of these same costumes are occasionally found on dolls and are especially delightful in miniature.

Play was now considered natural, and games and toys were common among middle-class children. Since trade with Europe was again vigorous, German papier-mâché and bisque dolls began arriving here in unprecedented numbers. In 1870 the Schwarz Toy Bazaar, forerunner to F.A.O.Schwarz, opened in New York City. It is considered to be the first toy-only store in America. Four Schwarz brothers had emigrated from Germany, each eventually opening a toy store, all stocked with the German items they knew so well. Since that time, their selection and presentation have delighted children and adults alike.

Department Stores and Mail Order Companies. Responding to all these new material needs of the Victorian family, enterprising and well-funded merchants began to build large department stores in major cities. Two extremely successful businessmen were John Wanamaker of Philadelphia and Marshall Field of Chicago. Department stores did not neglect the young; indeed, their catalogs show pages of toys and dolls available to amuse the children. Most of the dolls offered were imported from Germany and France, but the Parisian dolls were luxury items commanding substantial prices. Often doll heads of china and bisque were sold separately, allowing mothers to replace a broken part or revitalize a worn out doll. Occasionally, an old homemade cloth doll received a new store-bought head, but the original whole doll was left intact, its head simply stuffed up inside the new one; today it is a great treat to uncover such buried treasure. Importing only the heads saved shipping costs and stimulated American manufactures to produce cloth doll bodies which grew as a separate part of the industry. These manufacturers supplied importers and assemblers of dolls as well as mail-order companies like Montgomery Ward, who sold bodies in several sizes to coordinate with the available heads. A by-product of the mail order catalog was America's fascination with paper dolls; many little girls and their mothers cut out the figures and the fashions. Some young ladies made additional outfits for the dolls or were inspired to create their own original ones from this activity, which continued well into the 20th century.

Fairs and Expositions in the 1870s continued to be held in larger cities, both in America and throughout the world with dolls appearing in increasing numbers. At the 1875 Cincinnati exposition, Phillip Goldsmith, a local entrepreneur, showed dolls with his patented cloth bodies with built-on corsets. The following year, 1876, The Philadelphia Centennial Exposition featured numerous doll and toy entrants, including the New York Rubber Company, manufacturing under the Goodyear patent, Jacob Lacmann and Son, importers and assemblers, and E.R.Ives, showing mechanical toys. It was, however, the exhibit of Emile-Louis Jumeau of Paris that was most eyecatching, and which garnered him the Gold Medal. Most of the commercial dolls up through this period were in the form of ladies, long-necked, long-limbed creatures, displaying an adult demeanor that children were being instructed to aspire to even as they played. It was this type

of doll that Jumeau exhibited. His elegant lady dolls had bisque heads, and were dressed in elaborate au courant Parisian styles. Undoubtedly more than a few were bought by the mothers' to have their high fashion copied before becoming the child's best doll. Although dolls representing babies had been shown by the Japanese at the 1851 London World's Fair, and china and bisque head dolls with the proportions of an adult were often dressed as and played with as babies, a true revolution in doll design was just around the corner. Developed in France, the bébé, a doll representing a young child, with childlike proportions, and an innovative articulated composition body, was about to make its grand appearance. The child doll, in its myriad forms, was destined to virtually replace the lady doll in popularity within a few years. Anything the French can do, the Germans competed with, and Americans continued to be avid consumers of their great output.

Other exhibitions of dolls were noted through the end of the century, most of which were held to raise money for worthy causes. In 1876, a children's periodical, *Wide Awake*, sponsored a contest and exhibit in Boston in which the young readers were asked to dress dolls. Prizes were given in several age categories, up to 15, and the dolls were subsequently sent to children in hospitals for Christmas. A highly successful Charity-Doll Carnival, held in New York City in 1890, featured dolls dressed or contributed by First Ladies and other dignitaries and stage stars of the period. Ten thousand dolls were exhibited in Buffalo in 1896 and three thousand in Philadelphia the following year, with proceeds from these exhibits benefitting hospitals (*Collector's Encyclopedia of Dolls II*, Colemans). Certainly, recognition of the appeal of dolls was widespread, and other such exhibits were undoubtedly happening throughout the country at this time.

Patents and Patterns: Gender Trends. In the final decades of the 19th century numerous doll patents were granted in America. While some European patents were also filed here for protection, those that were given to American dollmakers are particularly interesting. As noted earlier, the first American doll patent was issued to Ludwig Greiner in 1858 for a method of making papier-mâché heads, very much in the German style of his forebears. Other patents soon followed, including several by men who combined clockwork mechanisms in toys incorporating dolls. In 1866, Dominico Checkeni patented a four-faced head which revolved vertically on an axis inside a molded wig-shaped frame, an ingenious technological wonder, of which the Strong Museum has three examples. Frank Darrow of Bristol, Connecticut received a patent for a process of treating untanned rawhide to mold as dolls' heads while he was manufacturing leather pulley belts for machinery. Joel Ellis and his collaborative in Springfield, Vermont patented wooden dolls with articulated mortise and tenon joints worthy of fine cabinetry, "with sufficient friction...to hold the limbs and body in any desired position." Several patents involved the doll assembly process, such as Jacob Lacmann's invention of inserting wire into leather fingers so they could be positioned and the hand then covered with leather to form a glove; Martin Kintzbach patented a method of attaching china hands to arms, using glue and cork, rather than needle and thread. Both Phillip Goldsmith and Charles Dotter each individually patented a cloth body with a printed corset which simplified production and eliminated some sewing. Thomas Edison's phonograph was only a decade old before he had miniaturized and adapted it to make a talking doll, using

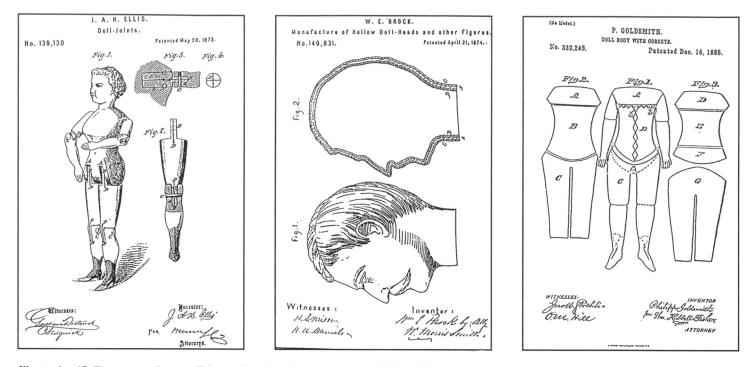

Illustration 17. Three patents by men. This sampling includes the wondrous 1873 Joel Ellis jointed wooden doll, the 1874 William Brock patent using leather for heads and the 1885 Phillip Goldsmith patent for cloth doll bodies having a corset and shoes.

imported heads and bodies. However, it was the 1892 patent for composition issued to Solomon D. Hoffmann, for Can't Break 'Em Dolls, that would ultimately mark the turning point in the American doll industry. Examples of these methods to "build a better mousetrap" can be found throughout the main body of this book. A masculine fascination with mechanisms is apparent in European patents as well, and indicated improvements to turn out a product faster and cheaper, using materials which were already available for some other purpose. Practical demands felt by the businessman-dollmaker seem to render him a businessman first, a dollmaker second.

During this same time period a number of patents for dolls were granted to women which also reflect a common theme. Almost invariably, the material of choice was cloth. Centuries of American mothers had made fabric dolls for their children, even when childhood was an abbreviated phase of life. It has been seen that children had much more freedom to romp and play through the end of the 19th and into the 20th century, the period of the bisque doll's greatest popularity. However, the fragile, breakable, ceramic material required more adult supervision and had surely injured many children in accidents. In addressing a need for safer dolls, the women had a natural choice, cloth. An exception to this is the 1865 patent of Lucretia Sallee, utilizing leather instead, shown on page 52. However, Sallee did address the concerns of other women, stating that her dolls were "constructed in such a way as to prevent them from being easily broken by a fall...". Such damage also occasionally hurt the child. Izannah Walker's 1873 patent is the first awarded for a cloth doll; her process involved sandwiching a thin layer of padding in between two layers of glued cloth, imparting a slight give to the face when touched. Her patent also attested that her doll was "inexpensive, easily kept clean, and not apt to injure a young child which may fall upon it." A concern for the child's safety is consistently noted in the doll patents granted women, and other dolls made commercially by women. These include Martha

Chase of Rhode Island, Martha Wellington of Massachusetts, Ella Smith of Alabama, Ida Gutsell and Celia and Charity Smith, all of Ithaca, New York, and Emma and Marietta Adams of Oswego, New York, women who were in the vanguard of their time.

The dollmaking enterprise of Martha Chase is well-documented in several books and articles, which give insight into her philosophy, motives and goals as well as the operation of her home workshop-business. These include Marjorie A. Bradshaw's *The Doll House: The Story of the Chase Doll* and *Dolls and Duty: Martha Chase and the Progressive Agenda* by Paul Bourcier and Miriam Formanek-Brunell, a publication from the Rhode Island Historical Society. The Strong Museum maintains an extensive collection of Martha Chase dolls and the molds which she used in their production, and many are shown on pages 99-103. Chase modeled some of her figures after literary characters from Charles Dickens novels and Lewis Carroll's *Alice in Wonderland*. Her George Washington is an excellent portrait, while her child dolls are simply endearing. Chase's aim was to produce dolls that were sanitary and soft, that looked and felt more like a child than the European bisque dolls, which she considered too heavy and awkward. Her goal was to create dolls that were lightweight yet durable, proportioned like real children, and that felt good to hold. Her ideas of what a child wanted and needed in a doll grew out of observing her own children at play, and were reinforced by the child-study groups which had become a movement in the latter decades of the 19th century. The sanitary aspect was of great importance to Chase; as a physician's wife (and daughter before that) she had an early knowledge of the relationship of cleanliness to health, which she stressed in her advertising. She was the voice of many women, mothers who also recognized that a child's imagination was fertile and flexible, and felt that simple toys stretched the imagination further than those which mechanically entertained. Like the men, middle-class women had their social roles well defined; situated primarily in the home, they

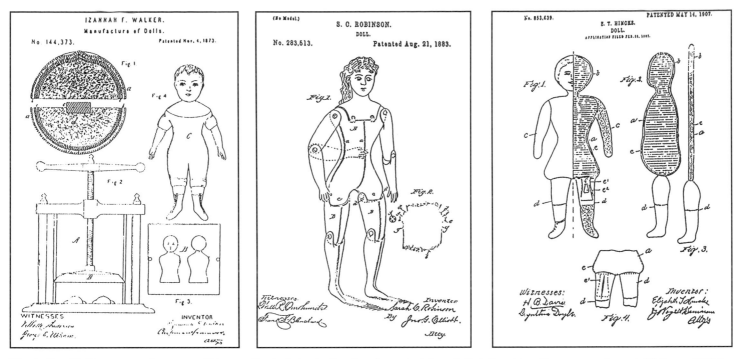

Illustration 18. Three patents by women. This sampling includes the first American patent for a cloth doll registered by a woman, Izannah Walker in 1873 for her painted cloth doll, the 1874 Sarah Robinson body of cloth with intricate articulations, and the heart warming 1907 Elizabeth Hinckes doll containing a hot water bottle filled through an opening in the leg.

drew on what they best knew, children and textiles. Dollmaking was readily complemented by their skills in needlework and painting. The natural result was that cloth dolls kept improving and became more professional. Thus, women entered a business that suited their talents and accentuated their training. Sirocco Productions recent video, "The Dollmakers: Women Entrepreneurs 1865-1945", was filmed in association with the Strong Museum and studies the work of over 30 women dollmakers. During the 20th century, with women and men working together on design and production methods, the American doll took form and soared.

Some down-to-earth concerns of women continued to be reflected in their doll patents and patterns. In 1907, Elizabeth T. Hincks of Andover, Massachusetts patented a cloth doll "with means whereby it may be heated and kept warm for a long period of time"—the means being a hot water bottle incorporated inside its hollow body, "and the child thereby enabled to enjoy the luxury of handling a warm doll instead of handling a cold doll with the attending liability of taking cold."

Toward the end of the century, a number of church ladies were busy with projects making and dressing dolls according to their chosen design. These dolls were sold to raise money for their churches or for missionary funds. Both the Moravian church of Bethlehem, Pennsylvania and the First Presbyterian Church of Bucyrus, Ohio, had active women's groups that made and sold thousands of dolls; an example of each is seen in *illustration 19*. The Moravian tradition has continued unbroken to the present day, while the Presbyterian ladies ceased production of their dolls for a period prior to 1950 and again in 1985 to the present. Although the face painting changes through the decades of production, the dolls retain their family resemblances, and speak now of a century of good works. Julia Beecher, wife of The Rev. Thomas K. Beecher of the Park Congregational Church of Elmira, New York is also noted for her endearing Missionary Ragbabies, made

of cotton or silk-jersey stockinette, with a combination of flat and needle sculpted hand painted features, one of which is featured on page 98. Julia Beecher was also the sister-in-law of reformers Henry Ward Beecher and of Harriet Beecher Stowe, adding further historical significance to these purely American creations. The tradition of making

Illustration 19. Two church ladies, the seated Presbyterian, ca 1900, wears a blue dress matching her oversized uplooking eyes. The Moravian, ca 1940, whose delicate features and hair only are painted, and not the entire head as with her counterpart, wears a classic pink checked dress and white apron. *Wenham Museum Collection, Massachusetts. Photo by Dorothy McGonagle.*

and selling dolls to benefit a worthy cause is an endeavor which continues today; one current example is the UNICEF doll which is designed to support the United Nations relief fund for children, internationally. A study of benefit dolls, worldwide, is a project currently being researched by the Doll Collectors of America, Inc., the oldest doll club in this country.

Imported dolls of the late 19th century. It is impossible and unnecessary to deny the beauty or the appeal of a French or German bisque doll, with its rosy complexion, idealized face, and human-like glass eyes and pearly teeth. With beautifully curled natural-looking hair that could actually be combed and dressed like perfectly ruffled little girls, these dolls epitomized the Victorian ideals of beauty. They were an enchanting tidal wave carried to our shore. But the concerns of the American mothers and dollmakers were real and many responded with great fervor; however, handwork and cottage industry cannot rival mass production. It would take a major change in direction and material for the American doll industry to begin to compete with the European imports; a change that would not happen until the 20th century.

Before the century ended, there were two more World's Fairs in America. The 1885 event in New Orleans was hailed as the greatest collection of American products ever assembled, but records list only two little known American dollmakers who participated. One was Mrs. M.M. Darrach who produced cornhusk dolls, which were definitely an American standard, but hardly an industrial wonder. Her dolls probably served as inexpensive souvenirs.

A festive fair also seemed an appropriate way to celebrate the 400th anniversary of the discovery of America. Thus, the World's Columbian Exposition in Chicago opened to the public in 1893 and was the spectacular culmination of only three years of official preparation, bolstered by a budget in the millions. In 1993, the United Federation of Doll Clubs held its annual meeting in Chicago, which had as its theme the "World's Columbian Exposition, Revisited". The souvenir journal from that convention contains a well-researched and interesting article by John Axe about the original Columbian Exposition, its evolution, buildings, participants, products, as well as numerous peripheral but intriguing details, such as the purse-snatching of noted social worker, Jane Addams, in the opening day crush. Among the entertainments available, the new-fangled Ferris wheel delighted fairgoers whose heads were spinning from the acres of exhibits. The Libbey Glass Company of Corning, New York exhibited a spun glass fabric called "fiberglass" which they used to dress a small Japanese composition baby doll, one of which is seen in *illustration 20*. Seventy-two countries participated in the event, including the notable European dollmakers. Jumeau presented an exhibit of large lady dolls in historical costume, while America saw entries of mechanical toys from Ives and novelties from E.I.Horsman, at this time primarily a distributor of toys, but with a growing interest in dolls. It was, however, the endearing hand-painted cloth dolls of Emma and Marietta Adams of Oswego, New York that stole the show. Awarded the Diploma of Merit, they became known as The Columbian Doll. A decade later, one particularly cosmopolitan Columbian doll would become quite famous, as we shall see.

The gay nineties continued...the first moving pictures were shown publically, and comic strips flooded the market. These fields would both come to influence dollmakers who reproduced the popular characters as either inexpensive novelty items or as significant dolls. The art of Charles Dana Gibson was becoming celebrated as

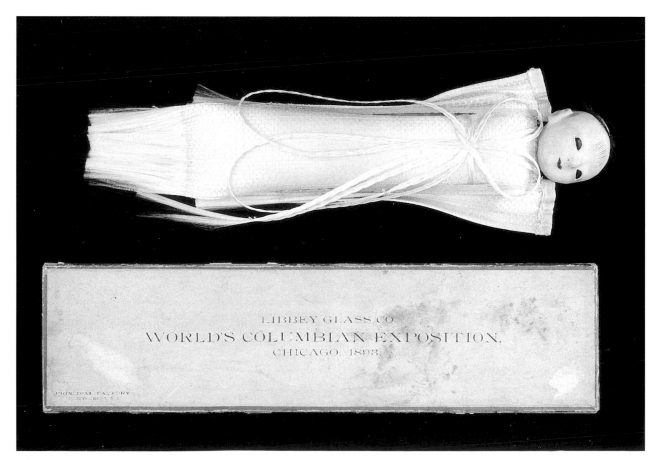

llustration 20. An innovative fiberglass-dressed Japanese composition baby doll (79.9746), 13-1/2in (34.5cm) sold by the Libbey Glass Company at the World's Columbian Exposition in Chicago in 1893, as marked on box lid.

well; his idealized representation of the classic American woman, the Gibson Girl, became recognized world-wide. She was slim with a stately elegance, haughty but personable, and crowned with a halo-like pompadour. She personified and symbolized the many roles American women of the Progressive era were coming to fulfill. The noted German dollmaking company J.D.Kestner produced an extremely fine rendition in bisque, which today is highly collectible. Numerous other individual doll artists from that time forward have found the subject tantalizing.

A study of children and dolls in 19th century America was undertaken by noted psychologists G. Stanley Hall and A. Caswell Ellis, both of Clark University in Worcester, Massachusetts. This extraordinary work has relevance to historians, child psychologists, doll collectors, and educators. In 1894 Dr. Hall had compiled and sent a questionnaire to approximately 800 teachers and parents requesting "juvenile feelings, acts or thoughts toward any object which represents a baby or a child" and asked for descriptions of anything that may have been regarded as a doll made of wax, rags, pasteboard, clothespins, vegetables, flowers, keys, etc. He further inquired about feeding, diseases, what constitutes a doll's death, names, accessories played with, sleep, discipline, or dress. Curiously, the question of dress had no fewer than twelve sub-questions such as "What is the influence of dolls upon the children?" and "Are children better morally, religiously, socially, or better prepared for parentalhood (sic) and domestic life by them?" Thousands of pages of detailed responses were received from 648 respondents, mostly from the United States, although a small percentage were from Scotland and England as well.

The magnitude of the response showed Hall and Ellis that the subject needed a careful and statistical study. Ellis therefore compiled a second questionnaire with 29 queries designed for briefer answers which could more readily be tabulated. This was sent to hundreds of school children. He received 845 responses to questions as varied as:

> Did you ever play with dolls? At what age did you begin and stop? Did you prefer playing with dolls alone or with other children? Did you prefer large or small dolls? Did you prefer your doll to be (and dressed as) a baby, a child, or an adult? This question was asked for ages 1 to 5, 5 to 10, and 10 to 15. Why did you stop playing with dolls? How did you punish your dolls? (at ages under six, and over six) Did you try to feed dolls, play that they were dead, think they were sick, cold, tired, hungry, good, bad, loving you, hating anyone? Which way of playing were favorites: dressing, washing or sewing for dolls, feeding, nursing, funerals or burials, doll parties, weddings, schools, punishing, putting to sleep, making companions to talk with?

These questions also elicited incredibly detailed responses; the returns and Ellis' previous conclusions were turned over to Dr. Hall, who supervised the tabulation and took responsibility for presenting the account of all the varied data and the added inferences. It was published by Hall and Ellis in 1897 as *A Study of Dolls*. Dorothy and Evelyn Jane Coleman reported on this study in *Dolls* magazine, March

1995, comparing Hall's observations to the dolls that have survived to today, a century later.

The study listed the order of preference for the material of dolls as wax, paper, china, rag, bisque, rubber, pasteboard, plaster of paris, wood, knit, with a few responses for a myriad of miscellaneous materials, which probably reflect what the parent could afford to provide and what the child thus knew. Hall's study also showed among other things that boys played with dolls and were partial to unusual ones like Brownies, Eskimo and Chinese dolls. It indicated younger children preferred dolls that represented babies, older children preferred child dolls, with adult dolls increasing in ratio, but still very much in the minority. The forms of doll play most reported were dressing dolls, washing them, having doll parties, sewing for them, playing school, putting to sleep, weddings, nursing, sharing companionship, followed by feeding, punishing and funerals. The five most frequently mentioned foods which were fed to dolls were milk, bread, cake, water, and candy, while forty odd items were each mentioned once, including buttons, brick dust and water, flour, grasshopper, mucilage and water, and soap suds. With such a diet, some of these dolls may not have survived! Considerable interest was noted in doll sicknesses. One doll with a toothache had her face broken by the child trying to pull the tooth. Others reported painting fevers on dolls with red paint, and one thought her doll with flaking paint had leprosy, a concept suggested by a Sunday School lesson. The most frequently listed sickness was measles, followed by scarlet fever, colds, whooping cough, diphtheria, injury, headache, mumps, chicken pox, sore throat, colic, croup, stomach ache and less commonly, biliousness, sore eyes, jaundice, chafed limbs and dyspepsia. Funeral play was mentioned on a substantial number of returns. One ten year old girl wrote: "We draped ourselves and the doll's coffin with crepe, it was a melancholy procession, and after a touching eulogy by my cousin, she was laid to rest beside the dead rooster." This child probably faced the death of someone close. Funerals were unfortunately a frequent part of children's lives, so doll burials would be one way for them to try and accept something all too common but beyond comprehension. Doll names showed great imagination and thought, and accessories included clothing, toiletries and household paraphernalia of every imaginable sort. One little girl commented that she wanted "two dolls, one to hit and knock about, and one for walks to show, perhaps a bride doll."

This exhaustive study confirmed the importance of dolls in child development a century ago which is still of interest today. Strong feelings were expressed by parents that children did indeed learn social and moral qualities, neatness and domestic skills from doll play and that this experience helped them in later parenthood. G. Stanley Hall affirmed the educational value of dolls in teaching subjects such as geography, history and even reading, noting that some children were motivated to learn in order to read to their dolls. The study documents the types of dolls and doll play that most influenced 19th century American children and also gives a solid reference point for research in the 20th century.

EARLY 20ᵗʰ CENTURY
A FLOURISHING AMERICAN DOLL INDUSTRY: COMPOSITION

The turn of the century. The U.S. census recorded that seventy five million people saw the new century arrive in America. The country was becoming increasingly more urban and American manufacturing was thriving. The automobile was being rapidly improved, and the Wright brothers opened a new dimension with their first successful airplane flight at Kitty Hawk, North Carolina, in 1903. That same year *Playthings* magazine began publication. Still in business today, *Playthings* provides a comprehensive history of the 20th century American toy and doll industry, documenting its early rapid development, which included manufactured cloth dolls and even more significantly, the increasing appearance of composition dolls.

Twentieth century composition dolls had been developing over the preceding decades, marked by the 1892 patent issued to Solomon D. Hoffmann, operating The First American Doll Factory. Definitions of composition can be confusing, since doll collectors refer to jointed bodies of several materials as composition, including combinations of wood and papier-mâché and plaster-mush mixes. Furthermore, some of the 19th century doll heads, such as Ludwig Greiner's, are generally called papier-mâché but technically are made of composition. Various mixtures of wood pulp, sawdust, glue, water, glycerine, zinc oxide, Japanese wax, and the like were mixed in secret formulas and patented by various manufacturers. All became nearly unbreakable when baked, although some were more susceptible to cracking and splitting or having their paint lift over time.

Two processes, cold press and hot press, were utilized. Cold press, the earlier method, was slower, requiring two days for setting and drying before parts could be removed from the molds. The more efficient hot press method used ganged metal molds, hinged like giant waffle irons, heated with steam or gas and forced together under great pressure to remove the moisture from the mix. Later, in the 1920s, parts were removed to electric ovens for more rapid drying. The major manufacturers of composition dolls in the early 20th century were Aetna for Horsman and the Ideal Novelty and Toy Company, which began operation in 1907 under Morris Michtom. Early Ideal production included celebrity dolls such as Ty Cobb and Dolly Varden. Horsman, as noted, was initially an importer who found his earliest doll success with the Billiken. Introduced in 1908, the Billiken statuette was promoted as a Chinese God of Good Luck and met with great success [*Illustration 21*]. The following year, the Billiken doll with a Can't Break 'Em head and cloth body was released by Horsman and sold over 200,000 in six months, according to *Playthings*.

Dolls of the People. In the early 20th century, the United States had become a recognized world power, and noted American individuals were represented in the dolls produced by German firms. Heubach created a sensitive, realistic portrait doll representing a Native American in bisque, and other companies soon followed. Of particular interest, too, are the Uncle Sam dolls mentioned on page 14, sometimes fitted with a music box which plays a patriotic American tune, and the George Washington seen in *illustration 22*. Also remarkable are the group of American naval officers and heroes

DESIGN.

F. PRETZ.

IMAGE.

APPLICATION FILED JUNE 9, 1908.

39,603.   Patented Oct. 6, 1908.

WITNESSES
M Cox.
L Kieof.

INVENTOR.
Florence Pretz
BY
F. G. Fischer
ATTORNEY

Illustration 21. The original design for Billiken was patented in 1908 by it's creator, an art student named Florence Pretz. She sold her rights to this squat, smiling good luck comic figure, reportedly for $60, and within two years Billiken proved himself to the manufacturer who had the great good luck to see production items clear a phenomenal million dollars.

produced by Cuno and Otto Dressel of Germany. The Strong Museum collection of six includes Admiral Dewey, Commander Sigsbee, and Rear Admiral Sampson, each a remarkable likeness of the officer represented, shown in *illustration 23*, along with a wonderful toy boat, the America.

Dolls by the People. Also during this time a number of creative artists, most of them women, became known for dolls which their artwork inspired and for dolls which they designed. Of particular note is Rose O'Neill, whose whimsical Kewpie drawings accompanied by stories and poetry became enormously successful. They were carried in *Ladies Home Journal, Woman's Home Companion, Good Housekeeping,* and the *Delineator,* and were followed by paper dolls called "Kewpie Kutouts", one of which is shown on page 77. Many other complementary characters fell from Rose O'Neill's imaginative pen, including the impish Scootles. A myriad of decorative items such as clocks, inkwells, talc containers, and doorknockers were based on O'Neill's drawings, many of which can be seen at the Strong Museum. Kewpie dolls were made in Germany of bisque, as well as in America of celluloid and of composition by the Cameo Doll Company of Joseph Kallus, and later of hard plastic and vinyl.

Madame Georgene Averill also designed dolls for the Averill Mfg Co. and later for Georgene Novelties. In addition to patenting

Illustration 22. George Washington astride horse which is a candy container (76.1854) from Germany, ca 1910. Overall height is 11in (28cm). Bisque head is marked only 16; the painted features capture the strength of the Father of our Country.

Illustration 23. Dolls of the American People include (left to right) the Cuno & Otto Dressel Naval heroes, Admiral George Dewey (76.856), Rear Admiral William T. Sampson (80.1219), and Commander Charles Dwight Sigsbee (80.1217), ca 1900. At 15 and 15-5/8in (38 and 40cm), they proudly stand before the lithographed battleship "America" (76.2030), patented July 24, 1877.

Illustration 24. The Three Graces...(left to right) Grace Corry's realistically expressive composition-headed girl with hair bow, a "genuine Madame Hendren doll", stands 14in (36cm) tall; Grace Storey Putnam's 13in (33cm) long BYE-LO baby perfectly captures the sweet vulnerability of the newborn, while the 10-1/2in (27cm) Campbell Kid designed by Grace Drayton is a whimsical character who retains the feel of the drawings from which she came. *Ursula Mertz Collection. Photo by Dorothy McGonagle.*

one of the first American mama dolls, she designed the capricious Bonnie Babe doll. The Three Graces are also significant and special: Grace Gebbie Wiederseim Drayton, Grace Corry Rockwell, and Grace Storey Putnam [*Illustration 24*]. Drayton's Campbell kids are as American as Campbell Soup, her September Morn an enchanting tyke, and her Dolly Dingle a household word. Grace Corry Rockwell's dolls exhibit a realistic child-like demeanor and fine character. Grace Storey Putnam is known for her newborn doll, the Bye-lo baby, modeled after an infant only days old. She was sculptural perfection and became wildly successful, known as the million dollar baby. Most of these dolls were produced in bisque in Germany through the distributor George Borgfeldt. Some versions were made in composition, celluloid or wax and are found on page 66. Additionally, a sampling of German-made bisque dolls designed by these talented American designers is included in *Illustration 25*. Many other women privately made dolls as artistic creations, based on magazine patterns or their own design, and some, like Emma Clear, became interested in faithfully reproducing elegant mid-19th century porcelain dolls as an expression of their talents.

Dolls for the People. The travels of Miss Columbia and the exchange of Friendship Dolls with Japan tell noble tales of American world-wide involvement, combined with American philanthropic goals. As mentioned earlier, exhibits of dolls were a means for

Illustration 25. Dolls by the American People include these German-made all-bisque charmers ranging from 4-1/2 to 6-1/2in (12—17cm). From left to right, they are Charles Twelvetrees' SHEbee (78.10755) from around 1925, Georgene Averill's 1926 Bonnie Babe (79.9763), Grace Storey Putnam's Bye-Lo baby (78.13887) from around 1925 in the bassinet, Jeanne Orsini's Vivi (78.10850) from 1920, and Rose O'Neill's Scootles (78.10727) from 1925.

women like Elizabeth Richards Horton of Boston to raise money for charitable causes. As the turn of the century approached, Mrs. Horton came up with the idea of sending one American doll, alone, across the country and around the world to be exhibited to raise money for children's causes, a mission that would be far more wide-reaching than she herself could attempt. The specially commissioned traveler was one of Emma and Marietta Adams' Columbian dolls, shown in *Illustration 26*. The United Federation of Doll Collectors 1993 convention journal contains an article about "Miss Columbia" by Diane D. Buck, then doll curator at the Wenham Museum in Massachusetts, where Columbia resides. Mrs. Horton had arranged for free transportation across the country through the Adams Express Company (no relation) and Wells Fargo and on April 12, 1900 "Columbia" left Boston. Her appearances were free to anyone who requested her presence, and the only stipulation was that at each venue a note be attached to Columbia's dress reporting the circumstances and amount of money raised at the exhibition. Columbia visited Chicago, Kansas City, and Denver among other cities as she traveled west. She was given a reception atop Pike's Peak and a dance in her honor at the

Southern Ute Indian Reservation in Nevada. She spent a year in California appearing at receptions, orphanages and benefits, and received gifts and souvenirs from children wherever she went. From California she traveled to the Phillipine Islands on the U.S. Army Transport ship, *Thomas*, which carried schoolteachers and soldiers to the new U.S. territory. Columbia spent a year there with her teacher-companion. In the autumn of 1902 Columbia was given passage on the transport McClellan and proceeded to sail westward around the world, visiting Hong Kong, Singapore, Ceylon, Malta and Gibraltar, finally returning to Mrs. Horton in Boston on Christmas Day, 1902, with all her gifts and stories. A journal accompanied Columbia and the entries written for her and about her in the course of her travels are remarkable, indicating how much this little American ambassador of goodwill touched the hearts of so many.

Twenty-five years later, the exchange of dolls between the children of the USA and Japan tell another story of good will and the spirit of friendship in a time of uncertainty. Collector and historian Phyllis Kransberg, who owns one of the Japanese Friendship dolls, shares this history:

"Dr. Sidney Gulick was a missionary stationed in Japan in the early 1900s. Upon his return to America, he was saddened to find much anti-Japanese sentiment, culminating in the Immigration Law of 1924 excluding Japanese from entering the USA. He then became the guiding force behind the Committee on World Friendship Among Children, spearheaded by the Council of Churches in America, for the exchange of dolls of friendship. Ultimately, 12,739 dolls of moderate cost were gathered by boys and girls in every state, guided by Sunday Schools, public schools, Girl Scouts, Campfire Girls, PTAs, etc. It was

Illustration 26. "Miss Columbia", a 19in (48cm) Columbian doll, ca 1899, was made by Emma Adams specifically for Elizabeth Richards Horton. Mrs. Horton's plan to have an American doll tour the world alone to raise money for children's causes was a feat accomplished by the determination and fervor of Columbia's supporters. She is seen here with her journal and some mementos acquired during her three years of travel. *Wenham Museum Collection, Massachusetts. Photo by Dorothy McGonagle.*

Illustration 27. Miss Kanto-Shu, 33in (84cm) tall, is one of the magnificent Japanese Friendship dolls sent to America in 1927 by the people of Japan in response to the flood of dolls sent to Japanese children from Americans through the Committee on World Friendship Among Children. *Phyllis Kransberg Collection. Photo by Dorothy McGonagle.*

sincerely hoped by Dr. Gulick and his committees that this project would foster lifelong friendships in the children's hearts. All 12,739 dolls were shipped to Japan courtesy of five shipping lines. Talking dolls, baby dolls, bride dolls, Red Cross nurses, Girl Scouts, boy dolls, dolls of dizzying variety, all traveled to their new little Japanese mothers. Each doll had a passport and a letter from the donor. They arrived in Tokyo on March 3, 1927, the date of Japan's important Doll Festival Day. In the presence of seven princesses of the Royal Family, ministers, and ambassadors, these tiny messengers demonstrated that the world can truly be one grand neighborhood of friends. The dolls were then distributed to children in the public schools of Japan.

Always recognized for their courteous manners, the Japanese people reciprocated immediately. Schoolgirls throughout the country contributed money towards a fund officially known as Doll Ambassadors of Goodwill. The most skillful Japanese artists were chosen to create 58 dolls which were 33 inches tall and dressed to represent the Japanese ladies of aristocracy, one of which is shown in *Illustration 27*. Their robes were made of the finest silks, decorated with delicate hand printed or painted patterns. Each doll was accompanied with elaborate accessories, such as a tea set, lacquer furniture, a trunk, a parasol, footwear, etc. After a six month tour through the United States, the dolls were then given permanent museum homes in each state.

From the guidance of Dr. Gulick to the enthusiasm of countless children, for that brief moment in the evolution of international history, dolls, just little dolls, succeeded as actual tangible resources for world peace and understanding."

In addition to the importance every doll acquires in sharing the love and growth of a child, the Friendship Dolls and "Miss Columbia" involved a multitude of people acting on their humanitarian concerns. They expand one's vision and reveal the many ways in which dolls have served as ministers "for the people".

20th Century Immigration. During the early part of the 20th century, a flood of immigrants entered this country. The neighborhoods set up by the immigrants resembled their old countries — little Italys, Germanys or Polands — and the traditions they brought with them to the New World included dolls from their homelands. Some impassioned photographs taken at Ellis Island show little girls clutching their beloved dolls, often comforting cloth companions.

The Period from 1910 to World War I. In 1910, *Playthings* reported: "For the first time in the history of toys, sales in American-made dolls, toys and games over the retail counter surpassed imports. Undoubedly, the advent of the American unbreakable doll was an important feature in this achievement..." A fim which joined the ranks of the American doll manufacturers that year was Fleischaker and Baum, who trademarked the name EFFanBEE in 1913. Among their early successes was Baby Grumpy, actually an endearing and enduring doll, which was carried in the line for fifteen years. They later employed important doll artists such as Joseph Kallus and Ernesto Peruggi, who designed a newborn baby to compete with the Byelo. When the United States entered World War I, the great wave of patriotism was reflected in the dolls produced here. Maiden America, shown in *Illustration 28*, was advertised as "The National Doll", and given as a promotional enticement with bond sales. Dolls of all sorts sported patriotic red, white and blue outfits, while nurses, soldiers, and Uncle Sams were ardent symbols of national pride. Anti-German sentiment meant that even some once-loved imported dolls were avoided and many were destroyed, further advancing the American doll industry. Two men of the period, Albert Schoenhut and Johnny Gruelle, helped fill that void.

The Albert Schoenhut Company. One of the most vital American dollmakers was Albert Schoenhut, who followed in the traditions of the German wooden toy industry. He emigrated to the United States in 1867 at the age of 17 and five years later opened his own factory in Philadelphia, making pianos and other toys. By the turn of the century he introduced his first circus, which was produced until 1935. These human and animal figures honed his wood turning and modeling techniques, which enabled his doll business, initiated in 1910, to reach a phenomenal level of success. Beautifully modeled and articulated, his All-Wood Perfection Art Dolls were eminently playable, not readily breakable (though capable of damaging other things or siblings), and washable, so they met several of the modern ideals. Schoenhut had six acres of factory space devoted to dolls and toys, representing the most prolific wood doll production in the world. Several examples are seen on pages 40-41, including a rare Santa Claus and sleigh, and the Gent Acrobat.

Raggedy Ann and Andy. John B. Gruelle was born in Arcola, Illinois in 1880. A man of many talents, he was a cartoonist for the *New York Herald* in his early career. Recognizing the nostalgic sentiment toward old things and the advantages of creating a homespun doll, he produced enough hand sewn "Raggedy Ann" dolls to secure a registered trademark in 1915, three years before his first volume of Raggedy Ann tales. The P.I. Volland Company produced dolls to sell along with the books. These comfortable, old-fashioned playthings became such a huge success that they have been reissued by various large doll companies throughout the century, including Georgene Novelties and Knickerbocker. A beautifully presented study of Gruelle and his work is seen in a recent video by Sirocco Productions entitled "Raggedy Ann and Andy: Johnny Gruelle's Dolls with Heart". Still being made today, Raggedys are known and loved by many a child...and adult alike.

Illustration 28. This winsome Patriotic mascot "Maiden America", a trademark registered to Katherine Silverman, is labeled The National Doll. She was produced in composition from 1915-1919 by the Maiden America Toy Mfg Company in New York City, and stands nearly 8in (20cm) tall, counting her topknot. *Dorothy A. McGonagle Collection.*

The '20s. The American dolls of the late teens and '20s show a profusion of styles reflecting the confusion of the times. Movie star replicas were created with a degree of artistry and reality that brought sculpture into the playroom. Novelty whimsies called beach dolls, described in a 1919 *Playthings* as "lovable...demonically delightful...plutocratic peaches of peerless pulchritude..." were available as well. Composition dolls made to look like German bisque dolls answered the needs of those who wanted a more "traditional" look, as seen in the products of the New England Doll Company, Artcraft and Mitred Box Company. A few American companies tried to compete with bisque, but their noble efforts are flawed. The unfinished white bisque heads of the Paul Revere Pottery seem to indicate production problems or other foibles; possibly someone forgot that the glass eyes they needed previously came from Germany. The Alexander Doll Company was established in the mid-'20s by Beatrice Alexander Behrman, who, as Madame Alexander, designed a line of cloth dolls with mask-type faces representing characters from literature, including her first of many versions of Alcott's *Little Women*, Carroll's *Alice in Wonderland* and several Dickens' characters. Later years would see Mme Alexander's composition dolls and costumes recognized as a benchmark of quality. Mama dolls, child dolls, baby dolls, flapper dolls, artist dolls, advertising dolls, celebrity dolls, bed dolls and dolls used as accessories that reflected adult interests...they were all part of the "what will they think of next?" '20s.

The '30s: The Great Depression. Panic and the crash of the stock market affected both the rich and the poor, resulting in massive unemployment. During the recovery, one of the numerous agencies formed under Franklin Roosevelt was the Works Progress Administration (WPA) which provided jobs for building schools and hospitals and commissions for artists, including dollmakers. WPA dolls and marionettes of cloth and composition were made in Wisconsin and other states and are discussed in Betty O'Sullivan's article "'Milwaukee's WPA Dolls" in the May, 1987 issue of *Doll Reader®*. Included is a newspaper photograph of Mrs. Eleanor Roosevelt taken in a Milwaukee toy shop where she was presented with two WPA dolls and quoted as saying "I simply love dolls." In Rochester, New York, a WPA project created a board game,Works Progress Action, which is seen in *Illustration 31*. The game consists of housing, bridge, highway and park projects which are completed by good and fortunate workers, reflecting American life in the 1930s.

Illustration 30. Johnny Gruelle's Raggedy Ann stories, from around 1915, spawned an interest in this loveable All-American doll that continues to this day.

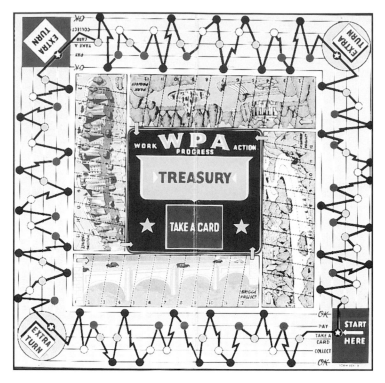

Illustration 31. WPA board game (91.1191) made in Rochester NY, ca 1934.

In 1932, the Winter Olympics were held at Lake Placid, New York—the third winter games, and the first in this country. One of America's ten gold medals was won by Sonja Henie for ladies' figure skating. After successfully repeating her performance in 1936, she turned professional and toured the United States in an ice revue, and appeared in a dozen movies. A tiny star with great appeal, Sonja Henie was a perfect subject for dollmakers. The official doll was produced by Madame Alexander, but other companies released lower priced versions to capitalize on her popularity, some of which were sold by Sears & Roebuck, whose catalogs provide a great deal of information on American culture.

The commercial dolls of the '30s reflect both the hard times and the escape that people sought through movies and inexpensive entertainment. Paper dolls were inexpensive and widely available in both cut-out books and in the newspapers. They even found their way into a very popular song, "I want to buy a paper doll that I can call my own." Mama dolls were also favored; these have composition lower limbs and cloth uppers which were sewn to a stuffed cloth torso containing a mama voice box. Their "swing legs" enabled a child to walk the doll, and many stores had doll company representatives dressed as nurses to teach the care of the doll to prospective little mothers. They reflect a return to more family-oriented values, a trend also seen in the Dy-Dee baby doll, which drank and wet. Madame Alexander capitalized on the sensation created by the birth of the Dionne quintuplets, selling the officially licensed and named dolls and assorted paraphernalia in remarkably large numbers, despite Depression-year hardships. Other companies cashed in on the phenomenon as well. Georgene Novelties expanded during this period to produce soft toys and dolls, perhaps answering a need for comforting playthings that was consistent with the times. The Effanbee Patsy doll, made of composition, is pensive and almost apprehensive, reflecting the prevailing attitude. Ideal's Shirley Temple (*illustration 33*), every mother's little girl, was presented as

both idol and icon and became the top seller in 1936 with sales of six million. June P. Kibbe, honorary curator of dolls and dioramas of the Boston Public Library recalls that she and some of her friends were not overly fond of Shirley because she smiled constantly and represented an unattainable ideal. She and Agnes Sura still wince at the memory of enduring the Saturday night regime of curling defiantly straight hair to effect a Sunday morning simulated Shirley Temple curly top. Effanbee's Patsy, on the other hand, was not so threatening and became a child's sympathetic friend, as recounted by author, collector and Patsy historian Nancy Carlson.

1939 World's Fairs and World War II. The '30s ended with the juxtaposition of two very dissimilar events. The World's Fairs, in San Francisco and New York, were a time of shared excitement and progress. In addition, they represented renewed hope, faith in recovery, and a time to move forward. Dolls were present at the Fairs and in shops to commemorate the events. *Illustration 34* shows a trio of young ladies, all fashionably dressed, who represent the promise of the time. One is a Joy Doll Corp. young lady, officially licensed for the New York World's Fair. Another is Madeleine de Baine from Madame Alexander, a doll released to represent a French fashion doll who, with her extensive wardrobe, was exhibited at the time of the Fair to raise money for charity. The French Madeleine originally was bought for a young American girl from Buffalo who traveled the continent in the 1870s with her family and on whom no luxury was spared. The doll, equally pampered, retains a magnificent wardrobe, articles of which were copied for adult fashions by Bonwit Teller in 1939. Portions of the proceeds from those sales also benefitted charity. The original Madeleine de Baine now resides at the Rosalie Whyel Museum of Doll Art in Bellevue, Washington.

The American spirit seen throughout the decade was reflected in the toy and doll industry. The Freundlich Novelty Corp. produced a series of dolls representing members of the armed forces. Their General MacArthur is fine portraiture; he is shown on page 127 with a WAAC and a WAVE. Paper dolls remained popular throughout the '40s, as well as baby dolls. Rubber was used for several popular drink and wet models, which also unofficially served to train girls for babysitting, the most frequent source of income for female teenagers. After the war, as the country returned to normal, civil rights issues began to grow more pressing. The National Pastime, baseball, brought a new level of awareness as the great African-American player, Jackie Robinson, was the first African-American to play in the major leagues. The doll modeled after him, in *Illustration 35*, was not just a symbol, it was a child's doll. This particular Jackie was really played with, has lost his hat, gotten dirty tagging home, and showed up for his photo without the Dodger name on his uniform. Jackie Robinson, the man, made heroic strides in furthering civil rights in America with the great strength and dignity he showed while becoming successfully integrated with the national pastime.

Illustration 32. Effanbee Doll Corp.'s first all-composition Patsy (74.207), ca 1928, designed by Bernard Lipfert, reflects a guarded simplicity with which little girls could readily identify. She stands 14in (35.5cm) tall, an easy size for child's play.

Illustration 33. Shirley Temple, the idealized little star who captured the hearts of many little girls and their mothers. Made by the Ideal Toy and Novelty Company, she kept their accounts in good order through a difficult decade. 11in (28.5cm) the small-sized Shirley was a favorite, then and now.

Illustration 34. This group of stylish young ladies from the late 1930s, include, from left to right, a 1938 Arranbee (80.607) stands 18in (46cm) tall, as does the Madame Alexander Madeleine de Baine (76.344), based on the exquisite and notable French lady doll who graced charity exhibits during 1937-1939. The smaller doll is 16in (40cm) and was produced by the Joy Doll Corp of New York. She was officially licensed as Miss New York (85.9010) for the 1939 New York World's Fair.

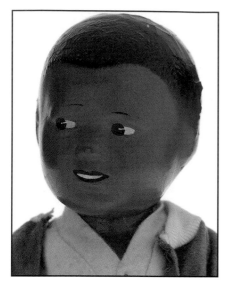

Illustration 35. Jackie Robinson, 1950s major league baseball player. Made by the Allied Grand Mfg Co, this 13in (33cm) doll (80.5204) has a composition head and body, painted brown eyes, and a gentle smile.

Illustration 36. Ballerina, Madame Alexander "Elise", ca 1958, 15in (38cm) has a hard plastic head and artistically posable vinyl body, along with the toe shoes in which her young owner once danced. *Rebecca M.C. Brignoli Collection. Photo by Dorothy McGonagle.*

MID 20TH CENTURY
DYNAMIC PLASTIC

1945-1970s. The Cold War years saw a tremendous development in the doll industry, due largely to the development and refinement of plastics. Television became a prime source of entertainment and inspiration. Americans saw Alaska and Hawaii become states and sports become mega-million dollar enterprises. All were ambrosia for dollmakers. The 1976 Olympic Gold Medal for figure skating was won by Dorothy Hamill, and this American heroine was immediately reproduced in miniature, as was her predecessor Sonja Henie, only now in plastic.

The dolls of this period tell many stories which have been revealed in a long-term, thoroughly researched exhibit presented at the Strong Museum entitled "When Barbie Dated G I Joe: America's Romance with Cold War Toys 1945-1970." Excerpts from the exhibit pamphlet note that:

"During the Cold War era, parents worked hard at preparing their children for adult life, particularly in teaching girls to be women and boys to be men... Few toys designed for children older than toddlers were gender-neutral...

The undisputed classic girls' toy of the Cold War era was the Barbie doll, introduced by Mattel in 1959 [*Illustration 36*]. Barbie was a textbook of lessons on proper female behavior. She taught preteen girls how to behave both as women and as shoppers...

Other popular girls' toys, like the Kenner Easy-Bake Oven, underscored domestic life...The girls at whom the advertising was aimed learned several things: that girls grew up to be moms and that mom's job was to be a homemaker as well as a mother; that moms — not dads — were in charge of baking; and that cakes were baked from mixes...

Toys helped market the atomic age...Atomic power provided the imaginary fuel for new toy trains, cars, and rockets. Manufacturers transformed old-fashioned chemistry sets into atomic energy labs. The atomic age influenced toy weaponry as well, as model missiles took their place alongside model ships on the toy store shelves. These popular toys acclimated children to the idea that atomic energy was the fuel of the future, and that atomic power could be safely and effectively harnessed and controlled."

In Cold War America, many children were afraid of the real world and readily imagined that we were "on the eve of destruction". The more carefree days of the early part of the century had passed, but the American family was intact, and still dreaming and planning. A look at the profusion of ballerina and bride dolls from the period acknowledges that dreams were okay, pretty was good, weddings were important, and becoming a bride, the desired and expected future for most girls.

The importance of plastic to the doll industry cannot be over emphasized. Malleable, lightweight, durable and efficient in the use of material and time, its application for dolls again revolutionized the industry. Inexpensive injection molding methods eliminated the need for heavy presses and heating equipment, and prolonged the lifespan of molds, while the dolls' skin coloration and texture improved dramatically. By the 1950s, the classic composition dolls,

Illustration 37. This formally attired Barbie doll (92.1399.3), ca 1961 by Mattel, wears the Enchanted Evening outfit from 1960-1963, which originally sold for $4.00.

the American standard, were outdated. The hard plastic and, even more so, the later soft vinyl dolls, fostered a creativity and realism in doll artistry which has continued to the present day. These new materials have also allowed elaborate and inexpensive toys to saturate the market. Although designed and sold by American companies, most of these dolls are no longer made in the United States. Because of their importance in the toy and doll industry both here and abroad, a brief overview of later 20th century dolls is included on pages 128-134.

The little eight-inch child dolls epitomized by the Vogue Doll Ginny appeared throughout this period and have seen a resurgence in today's market. The 1950s Ginny wore a synthetic wig which could be washed and curled like real hair, and replaced when worn out or cut too short, as well as a wardrobe that duplicated everything a little girl herself could possible want. Ginny played, roller-skated, went to school, attended church, and ran into rain puddles. She posed as the Coronation Queen, representing Queen Elizabeth II, in one of the first televised historical events in this country and became one of the most popular dolls of the period, inspiring numerous look-alikes. The Vogue Doll company, started in 1939 in Medford, Massachusetts by Jennie Graves, introduced the older boy companion doll, Jeff, in a 1955 brochure with the greeting, "Hi, I'm Jeff, it's tonic time...." In comparison to Ginny, Jeff was only moderately popular, but perhaps he was a little misunderstood. In Massachusetts, the word "tonic" does not refer to a medicine as in other parts of the country. Instead, it is the local term for a carbonated soft drink, still used today. The Vogue Doll company is an excellent example of a modern, successful cottage industry which employed as many as 800 women, working at home. They produced quality items according to their own schedules which enabled them to both care for their families and work.

The final decades of the 20th Century have seen a myriad of dolls produced primarily in vinyl, which reflect the conflicting values of the past fifty years. Many have already been well-researched by doll historians whose articles and books thoroughly document this period. These decades, however, could be analyzed quite thoroughly by historians of the future if they had only Barbie, and perhaps Ken dolls, to guide them. Through her nearly forty years Barbie has held every job available to women, from her early years as homemaker and shopper, nurse, teacher, ballerina, telephone operator, perpetual prom queen, businesswoman, stewardess, doctor, to jet pilot and astronaut. The 1993 Air Force Barbie doll in *Illustration 38* is a Pentagon-approved Captain, the play doll of the young daughters of the late Capt. Scott Ward, U-2 pilot, whose memory she salutes. In representing American life, Barbie doll has no equal.

The last quarter of the 20th century has also seen a continuation of the fads and crazes of a rapidly changing culture, all too frequently represented in the American toy market. Toys reflecting the current movies appear in stores the moment the film or video is released. The pervasiveness of television in children's lives has extended peer pressure and has led advertisers to aim directly at the children. Gone are the ads geared toward parents: "If Stradivarius had made dolls, he would have made the Chase Stockinet Doll." Action figures such as the Power Rangers appear almost overnight and sweep the country causing a dawdling parent or grandparent to miss out on buying the "right" color or power resulting in inconceivable disappointment. Grotesque and powerful fantasy figures, some of which almost defy description, introduce supernatural forces to children they can only dream of or pretend to possess. Fortunately, the most favored seem to be the "good guys", for the forces of evil are more sinister than ever before. Collector and researcher Fred Sura points out that in the factory packaging and output, the ratio of "good guy" action figures to the villains is significantly higher, bearing up this positive aspect. With their superhuman abilities, my husband Jerome comments that these figures are strangely evocative of the talismans and idols of the ancients.

Children seem to have a renewed interest in dolls that crawl, eat and wet, although these infant behaviors are present in every generation of dolls. Batman and Barbie co-exist, but while the one is basically boy-oriented and the other girl-oriented, observation of my young nieces and nephews show an easier crossover in play. During the past two decades there have been some subtle changes in the doll world, including the appearance of the soft and cuddly Cabbage Patch dolls. These were originally designed and produced during the 1970s in small numbers as handmade cloth babies by Xavier Roberts, operating as the Original Appalachian Artwork, Inc. They were as different from the homemade centuries-old cloth dolls as

Illustration 38. 1994 U.S. Air Force Captain Barbie appears to be "out of regs," sporting a ring and earrings though she has kept her hair within length limits. There are apparently no hair width limits in Regulation 35.10. *Doll courtesy of Jayme and Brooke Ward. Photo by Dorothy McGonagle.*

they were from Raggedy Ann. In 1983 they were released in vinyl by Coleco to a world of children, boys and girls, some merely babies themselves, eager to adopt and love these funny-faced individuals in universal affirmation of the doll as a nurturing toy. One of my six year old informants insists that boys do not play with "dolls", while another is equally adamant that "boys have to be the daddies." Perhaps with many modern fathers sharing in childcare responsibilities, attitudes toward doll play have likewise shifted. Studies indicate that children frequently choose gender-specific toys by the age of three, but they learn from what they live with as well as from the messages inherent in the toys used in their play.

Patriotism is fashionable again, so historically costumed dolls are more apparent, just as military dolls were popular during and after the 1992 Persian Gulf War. Also, as previously mentioned [on page 12], a symbol of respect for times past is seen in the American Girls series of dolls, which teach today's children the experiences and values of the past that have made America strong. Seen in *Illustration 39* is a model American child, Claire Castle, with her Samantha doll.

Strong Museum Doll Oral History Project. Recognizing the importance of dolls in our culture, in 1987 the Strong Museum undertook a research project, called the *Doll Oral History Project*, in which a number of women were questioned about their doll play as children. It was similar to G. Stanley Halls' questionnaire for children conducted at the end of the 19th century, and many of the adult recollections were the same as the children had reported. The importance of doll play should not be underestimated, and an understanding of the ways in which children relate to their dolls is tantamount to understanding the child. As noted, American doll collectors and museums have long recognized the historic and educational value of dolls and have endeavored to preserve that history for future gener-

ations. The doll collection of the Strong Museum is acknowledged to be the largest public collection in the world, and the task of maintaining and interpreting it as part of the broad fabric of American life remains an ongoing commitment.

As the 20th century draws to a close, it is interesting to reflect on the billions of dolls there are in America, and of all the purposes they have served. Many men and women collect antique dolls because of their fascination with history. Others love the artwork, and so are drawn to the original artist dolls that are sculpturally superb, but were made for collectors, not as playthings. The dolls of Dorothy Heizer and Martha Thompson fall into this category and are included in this study as representative of that endeavor. However it is the play doll of yesterday cherished by collectors today, along with the dolls of today cherished by children in play that have been the primary focus of attention here. As you browse through the pages of this book and ponder the vast variety of dolls embraced here, I hope they will spark memories, make you ask questions, or encourage an appreciation for the American doll. These selections from the Strong Museum's collections are all representatives of America, each in its own way.

Despite the ever-changing variety in dolls, those that remain classics are the simple dolls that stimulate imagination. They are baby dolls, hugged by little children who relate to them and child dolls, played with by older children who teach them. Domestic skills are learned whether intended or not, and dolls representing the peoples of all nations, of all colors, continue to live in the homes of today's child. These are the dolls of America. Of any material, the American doll exhibits a certain grace and strength. It has become a bellwether, and its story, in the telling, becomes a celebration of the American people.

Illustration 39. A peek at some children and dolls spanning the 20th century includes Margaret Woodbury (later Strong) playing with her German bisque doll and her American Babyland cloth doll in 1903, Bob Cairns in 1944 with his sister Dorothy's long lost baby doll and Claire Castle in 1995 with Samantha, the Pleasant Company doll representing the Victorian era.

WOOD

PRIMITIVE OR FOLK ART DOLLS

Play dolls made of wood predate written history. A simple forked stick readily lends itself to becoming a doll. Ancient graves throughout the world have yielded decorated sticks, which, when wrapped in grass, tow, or other softening materials, allow even the most primitive talent to create a head. Thus, a doll is born. However found, whether as simply embellished sticks, retooled discarded household objects such as spoons or clothespins, or beautifully carved and jointed figures, the quality of wood holds a special charm. Many of these antique and semi-antique figures hint at the love of a father or grandfather expressed with a jackknife and a desire to please a child.

Illustration 40. These five hand-made wooden dolls capture and arouse a range of emotions. Generally a content group, they are probably all early 20th century except for the simple lathe-turned, skittle-shaped doll (73.1461), whose wood suggests mid-19th century. She seems bigger than her 11-1/2 inches (29.5cm). The more sophisticated African-American woman (80.5029) with the gently carved, expressive face has a cloth-covered wire armature body, enabling a stooped posture. One lady (75.518) is sporting a hat, another (79.9712) curly hair, a glue and sawdust composition applied to her head and painted. The laminated lady (79.9727) with high-heeled shoes and nipped in waist has a fur pieced wig and nail heads for eyes.

Illustration 41. A mere 6 inches (15cm) this carved wood Native American doll (79.9704) dates from around 1830. Representing a male Menominee from the Great Lakes region, this doll has traces of facial paint characteristic of a warrior. The doll's round tin chest ornament is similar to the silver chest ornaments some Natives wore to protect the heart from malevolent influences.

Illustration 42. Mid 19th to mid 20th century Folk Art Wooden Dolls. They range in size from the 9in (22cm) baby carved from a single piece of wood (79.9717) to the African-American (79.9713) at 15in (38cm). Clockwise from him is a carved hair lady (79.9716) with paper features and clothing cut from a magazine. In front of her is a 19th century primitive lady, 15in (38.2cm), in a red dress (79.9723). Standing beside Pinnochio, 17-1/4in (43.8cm), (79.9731) is a glass eyed boy, 13-1/4in (33.5cm), in a brown velvet suit (73.1476). The man, 15-3/4in (40cm), behind him was artistically carved in detail (79.9732). Directly above him is a gentleman, 12in (31.2cm), with oversized hands and white beads for eyes (79.9711). Next to him is a lady, 11-1/2in (29.4cm), with painted features (79.9702).

37

Illustration 43. Carved wooden head dolls with painted features, the Eskimo man (76.741) is signed E.D.Hunnicut, and the woman Burton Sours at Kotzebue Alaska July 14, 1938. Just over 16 inches (42cm), both wear fur parkas, fur and leather boots; the woman (76.740) also has a printed cotton dress under her parka.

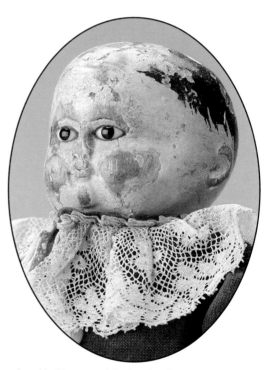

Illustration 44. Close up of the boy in *Illustration 42* shows a 13in (33.5cm) doll (73.1576) with a sweet simplicity. Probably second half of 19th century, he has the look of the commercial German and American round-faced papier-mâché dolls or is influenced by the so-called Motschmann-type dolls, sparked by the Japanese baby introduced to the world in 1851. He has carved wooden hands and head with glass inset eyes, painted hair, and a cloth body.

Illustration 45. Early 20th century folk doll (80.5029), detailed from *Illustration 40*. Standing 12-1/2in (32cm), she has a sensitively portrayed expression.

SPRINGFIELD WOODENS

The rock maple dolls of Springfield, Vermont, were produced from 1873 to 1893 by a number of men who made almost continuous modifications, mostly to accommodate production. Begun by Joel A. H. Ellis, who manufactured carriages and toy carts, production was carried on by Frank D. Martin, Dexter Martin, George W. Sanders, Henry H. Mason, Luke W. Taylor, Charles C. Johnson and D. M. Smith, among others. The intricate jointing was considered the chief merit; an advertisement reprinted in the 1940 Doll Collectors of America Manual proposes the jointed doll to be of such interest to children that the "cost and trouble of dressing" could be avoided. These slope-shouldered dolls could survive rough play, though most surrendered their paint to the cause. Like so many 19th century American production dolls, they retain the look of the German china and papier-mâché dolls of the period. Because parts and partnerships were interchanged, identifying any particular doll as to maker and patent has always been a challenge to collectors and has encouraged the use of the generic term "Springfield Woodens".

Illustration 46. A primitive woman (79.9719), probably early 20th century whose glistening unpainted body bears remarkable likeness to the 1880s Springfield wooden, 10 and 12 inches (25.4 and 30.5cm) tall. The Springfield doll (75.5500) reflects a combination of several patents taken out by the collaborative group of men in Vermont: the Martin hip, the improved ball and socket knee of Sanders and Johnson's added neck piece.

Illustration 47. This 1882 Springfield doll (75.5500) of multi-heritage is paired with an 1873 patent Joel Ellis wooden (78.1164) in the larger 15 inch (38.5cm) size. Both are seated in a carriage which is stamped ELLIS under the seat. Before making dolls, Joel Ellis manufactured toy carts and carriages; it is satisfying to see one carrying one of his dolls.

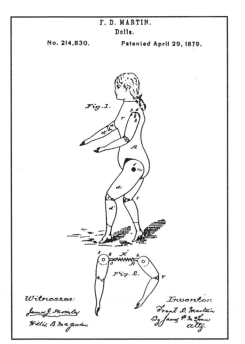

Illustration 48. 1879 Frank D. Martin doll patent.

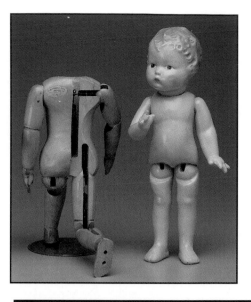

Illustration 49. The salesman's sample of the Schoenhut body (74.180), standing at 12in (31cm), demonstrates the patented spring system which gives it the ability to hold positions so nicely. It also shows the two holes in the bottom of the feet which fit securely over a pin in the metal stand Schoenhut made for the dolls. Socks are made with a bound-open sole while the shoes have two grommets to accommodate the stand. Also shown is the 1930 composition bodied doll (84.149) 13 inches (32.5cm), who is also seen in the composition section on page 124. She was designed by Harry Schoenhut, has a bent right arm typical of some composition dolls of the period, notably Patsy, and represents the last doll designed by the firm.

Illustration 50. These three babies illustrate offerings from the Schoenhut firm. Left, the wood-bodied, ca. 1915, "Nature Limb" baby body (78.3273) with bent limbs and fat rolls was offered through most of the production years, as infant dolls gained in popularity throughout the teens and early twenties. Center, a replica of the phenomenally received Bye-lo baby (78.3278) 15in (38cm) designed by Grace Storey Putnam and distributed by Geo. Borgfeldt & Co., was produced in very limited numbers under Harry Schoenhut in 1925. They have been found on several body types probably produced outside the company, such as this stuffed cloth frog-leg body with celluloid hands. An explanation suggested by Ruth and Robert Zimmerman in *Doll Reader®*, June/July 1985 is that Schoenhut, who maintained a business relationship with Borgfeldt, began a venture that did not proceed, for this doll appears in no Schoenhut catalogs. The 16in (40.6cm) doll (77.707) on the right, from around 1924, is one of Schoenhut's "Stuffed Dolls with Mamma Voices". Her hollow wood head swivels on a wood shoulderplate, she is relatively lightweight and comfortable to hold, and she follows the rage of the mid to late 1920s.

Illustration 51. The Schoenhut carved hair dolls are often deeply sculpted and full of character, especially those of the early years. The hair styles are numerous, some quite elaborate and others simple realizations of children. Seen here are a 14-1/2in (37cm) tall bonnet-headed girl (78.3253) from 1912 with wonderfully carved wisps of hair peeking out from under her cap, a 1911 girl (78.3255) at 15-1/2in (39cm) tall, designed by M. Graziano in the initial production year, and a classic boy (88.1226) with short, light brown hair, from about 1915. He stands 16in (41cm) tall. All wear the union suits which were part of every Schoenhut's basic wardrobe.

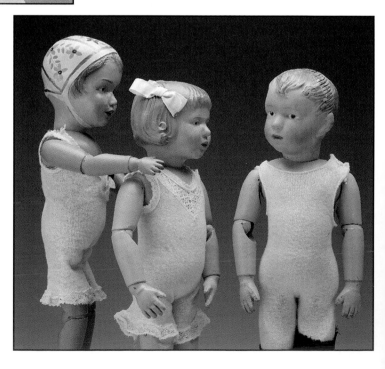

SCHOENHUT

When Albert Schoenhut immigrated to America in 1866, he was part of the third generation of a German toymaking family. He entered into a German-American community where he could use his skills to contribute to the growing toy and doll industry centered in Philadelphia. His natural affinity for wood first found expression in the manufacture of toy pianos, for which he formed his own company in 1872, at the age of 23. In 1908 he built a six story factory with almost six acres of floor space, which was advertised as the largest and best equipped in the world. Almost four decades of production of musical instruments and toys, circus figures and animals preceded the patenting and presentation of his Schoenhut Perfection Art Doll in 1911, a wooden jointed marvel with steel springs.

After Albert's death in 1912, his six sons, headed by the eldest, Albert F., carried on the A. Schoenhut Company. While the dolls, made until the 1930s, are found with a variety of eye treatments, carved hairstyles or separate wigs, they all gently depict real children with lifelike expressions. An encyclopedic study of the firm, its progressive offerings, and the subtle nuances within each product line, can be found in *Schoenhut Dolls* by Carol Corson. The Strong Museum has a fine and varied collection of Schoenhut dolls and toys. Poseable, playable, and eminently charming, the Schoenhut doll stands alone as the early 20th century's foremost American wood doll.

Illustration 52. "Oh You Beautiful Doll". This extremely lovely girl (78.3283), circa 1915, seems to be contemplating bursting into song. She is the classic essence of a Schoenhut doll, and at 21 inches (54cm), she is the largest size made. Her lovely original blonde mohair wig suits her perfectly and retains its freshness of style. Above the piano keyboard the printed paper decorations show three winged cupids and the Schoenhut trademark medallion.

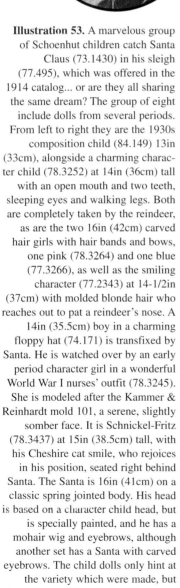

Illustration 53. A marvelous group of Schoenhut children catch Santa Claus (73.1430) in his sleigh (77.495), which was offered in the 1914 catalog... or are they all sharing the same dream? The group of eight include dolls from several periods. From left to right they are the 1930s composition child (84.149) 13in (33cm), alongside a charming character child (78.3252) at 14in (36cm) tall with an open mouth and two teeth, sleeping eyes and walking legs. Both are completely taken by the reindeer, as are the two 16in (42cm) carved hair girls with hair bands and bows, one pink (78.3264) and one blue (77.3266), as well as the smiling character (77.2343) at 14-1/2in (37cm) with molded blonde hair who reaches out to pat a reindeer's nose. A 14in (35.5cm) boy in a charming floppy hat (74.171) is transfixed by Santa. He is watched over by an early period character girl in a wonderful World War I nurses' outfit (78.3245). She is modeled after the Kammer & Reinhardt mold 101, a serene, slightly somber face. It is Schnickel-Fritz (78.3437) at 15in (38.5cm) tall, with his Cheshire cat smile, who rejoices in his position, seated right behind Santa. The Santa is 16in (41cm) on a classic spring jointed body. His head is based on a character child head, but is specially painted, and he has a mohair wig and eyebrows, although another set has a Santa with carved eyebrows. The child dolls only hint at the variety which were made, but show the posable and playable nature of the Schoenhut doll, not only for the children of yesterday, but for children of all ages. Albert Schoenhut was known as the Santa Claus of Kensington, his area of Philadelphia. With the delight his toys provided, it is easy to understand why!

there arose such a clatter"...

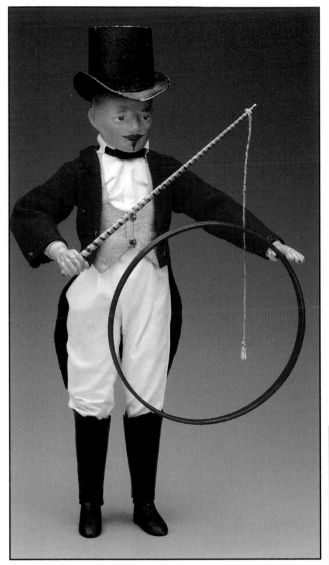

SEGMENTED WOODEN

Segmented wooden toys have existed for centuries, originating in many cultures as crude wooden and ivory carvings or beads strung together to form puppetlike articulations. Simple jumping jacks made of paper or wood were an extremely popular child's toy, fancied by adults as well, in the 17th and 18th centuries. The first half of the 20th century found a great revival of this production technique while the use of elastic for stringing together separate wooden body parts enhanced the qualities of poseability and animation, as seen in Schoenhut's circus figures. Stellar designer Joseph L. Kallus created many wonderful and inexpensive celebrity figures in the segmented wood form, drawing inspiration from humans, animals, cartoons and movie animation, as well as the advertising world. Kallus began his long career in the doll design field when, as an art student in 1912, he was chosen by Rose O'Neill to assist in the development of her phenomenally popular Kewpie dolls. He formed the Rex Doll Company in 1916, and following military service, the Cameo Doll Company in 1922. While his name is inseparable from Cameo, many of his designs were produced by other companies.

Illustration 54. This marvelous Schoenhut dates from c. 1915, and represents the Ringmaster (73.3481). Standing 19in (48cm) tall, his body is that of the Manikin, with a joint at the waist, enabling him to bend and twist. He also has a uniquely modeled right hand which holds a whip.

Illustration 55. Betty Boop (73.1351), Popeye (80.4618), and Minnie Mouse (79.4642) were rendered by Joseph Kallus from animated cartoons. Betty Boop's design was copyrighted by Fleischer Studios in 1932; she stands 11-1/2in (30.5cm). From Walt Disney came Minnie Mouse (79.4642), 12in (31.1cm) and Popeye (80.4618) 5in (13cm), King Features Syndicate, Inc, 1940, who remain popular characters even today.

Illustration 56. A parade of segmented wooden dolls produced by Joseph Kallus includes "Selling Fool", the 16in (41cm) RCA Radiotron (76.440), early 1930s, from a design by the artist Maxfield Parrish. Moving clockwise, the 19in (48cm) GE Radio Man called Bandy (76.442), 1929, both produced by the Cameo Doll Co, a 14in (32cm) King Little III (77.2570), produced by Ideal Toy and Novelty Company, from Max Fleischer's design for "Gulliver's Travels," 1939 Paramount Pictures, Walt Disney's Jiminy Cricket (80.4628) 8in (21cm), made by Ideal in 1940 and Pinocchio (77.2567), 1939, made by the Knickerbocker Toy Company.

19TH CENTURY PAPIER-MÂCHÉ/COMPOSITION

Despite our use of the French name, papier-mâché was developed by the Chinese and used as a moldable material for everything from small objects to furniture. Dolls have been made of papier-mâché for centuries. The concoctions used in its manufacture varied greatly and individual formulas were often guarded by their producers. Some are basically laminated paper sheets, others a paper mush mixed with an assortment of materials such as gypsum, plaster, various glues, cloth fibers, sand, clay, sawdust, lime, salt, and borax. You name it, someone has tried it. The foremost manufacturers of papier-mâché dolls in America were German immigrants who brought their trade, often even tools and supplies to America. Their dolls look much like their German forebearers. Most of the American papier-mâché dolls were patented for the specific process of manufacture. Ludwig Greiner, who received the first doll patent in America, simply reinforced the heads with cloth, an extra production step that made them more stable and less vulnerable to hard play.

Toward the end of the 19th century, papier-mâché became an inexpensive material because daily newspapers were common and were easily recycled. Early paper contained more coarse wood and rag fibers, so as an inexpensive scrap it tended to make a much stronger pulp than today's waste paper. As other materials were added and the proportion of paper became less, the material is referred to as composition. There were many small companies in America making such dolls; examples from the Strong Museum included here are by Ludwig Greiner, Judge and Early, Lerch & Co, Emma Bristol and Webber, as well as a marvelous prosopotrope patented in 1866 by Domenico Checkeni.

LUDWIG GREINER

Ludwig Greiner, one of the principal and earliest American manufacturers of doll heads, immigrated to this country in the 1830s. Like many other German craftsmen, his family settled in Philadelphia, where he operated a toy and doll business from 1840 until his death in 1874. His sons continued the business until 1884. Greiner's 1858 patent for reinforcing papier-mâché doll heads with cloth is the first to be granted in America, and includes his formula for one pound of white paper, cooked and beaten, to which is added one pound each of dry Spanish whiting and rye flour, plus one ounce of glue. It is easy to recognize the heads, when they bear one of several versions of his label, dated either 1858 or with the patent's extension date of 1872.

Pre-patent examples are harder to document, but many unmarked heads may, in fact, be from the Greiner workshop. Identification requires a close study of painting techniques. The patented heads show a great variety of hairstyles and range in size from "0" at 13 inches to size "13", almost 36 inches. Most of the heads had painted eyes, generally a deep teal blue bordering on black or, more infrequently, brown. Dark glass eyes are rare, but have been found on an occasional 1858 head. Good quality oil paints were used for the flesh tones and features, and a coat of varnish protected the finish. While the varnish has, over the years, tended to yellow, a remarkable number of these dolls have survived in good condition. Heads were either sold separately for stuffed cloth bodies made at home, or complete dolls were made available for the consumer.

Many Greiner heads are found on bodies made by Jacob Lacmann, which he patented in 1871 and 1874. They are made of cloth with fingers formed of wire and hands covered with leather like a glove; the later version had a papier-mâché hand and heeled foot underneath the cloth. Apparently, Greiner and Lacmann had a personal, as well as a business relationship evidenced by Lacmann's witnessing Greiner's will. A sampling of the Strong Museum's Greiner dolls attests to their diversity and appeal.

Next Page: Top: **Illustration 57.** These two dolls show the dramatic differences in hairstyles from the 1858 period to the 1872 patent extension era. The Greiner on the right (79.4234) a 22in (56cm) doll has a childlike demeanor, dark hair with a deep center part and short wisps of hair curling onto her forehead. Typical of the early dolls, she has eyelashes on the upper lids, and soft pink mouth coloring. The label on the blonde doll (79.4233), which stands at 25in (63cm), has the addition EXT 72, denoting the seven year extension granted Greiner on his patent. The label is also marked with the size number, 6, but it is her light hair coloring and swept back style that first identifies her later age. The eyes are a lighter blue and there are no eyelashes, but instead has a red line over the eyelid. The mouth painting is red. Both have cloth bodies with kid arms. *Bottom:* **Illustration 58.** Two sturdy Greiner dolls with the label Greiner's Improved Patent Heads Pat. March 30th 1858. On the left, a 29in (74cm) dark-haired lady (79.4244) with center part and hair pulled behind ears with long curls across the back. Her eyes are painted a very deep blue. The smaller doll is 23-3/4 inches (60cm) and has the rarer glass eyes (77.2339) that are soft black. Her hairstyle is quite similar but the curls are shorter. There are often subtle differences in the hairstyles, but most of the 1858 dolls have dark hair, almost invariably with a center part. This lovely doll holds a charming roly toy in the shape of a doll who looks quite like a Greiner, but is possibly German. Both have cloth bodies with white kid arms.

57.

58.

Illustration 59. Products of Philadelphia neighbors, the 24in (61cm) man is a Greiner (79.4242) simply stamped "PATENT HEAD" on the back of his shoulder, which would date him at just about 1858. He is rare, with black pupiless glass eyes and upper lashes. His cloth body has kid lower arms with wood separated fingers, and he wears a handsome outfit complete to his black kid shoes and his black beaver high hat, with its Victor Jay and Company London shop label. His companion (79.512), also rare, is by Philip Lerch. She is 23-1/4 inches (58.5cm) and has a cloth body with mitt hands.

Illustration 60. Lovely Lerch lady (79.512), at 23-1/4in (58.5cm) in height, is a seldom found doll. Philip Lerch was one of the many Philadelphia dollmakers; he was listed in the directories from 1858 to 1879. This doll has classic black molded hair pulled behind her ears and blue painted eyes.

Illustration 61. Lerch label (79.512) and early Greiner stamp (79.4242) from the dolls in *Illustration 58*.

Illustration 62. Other manufacturers of American papier-mâché or composition doll heads include, standing left, a center-part blonde, 26-1/2in (67cm) c. 1875, (79.8229) with a label reading American Muslin-lined Head No 6 Warranted Fast Oil Colors. These heads have been found on various commercial and homemade bodies, this a stuffed cloth of the Philip Goldsmith type. The other two dolls, (80.1725) from about 1875 and (83.679) 1882 respectively, are unmarked but are very similar to marked Judge and Early dolls; their distinctive hairstyles suggest they hail from that Philadelphia and Baltimore operation. Edward S. Judge received a patent for coating molds in 1868 and another in 1875 for the manufacture of papier-mâché heads. His association with Early is unclear, with a listing only for one year, 1875; perhaps it was in some way related to the patent granted that year. The dolls are unusual and attractive, clearly deserving of the attention they receive. All have cloth bodies with kid arms.

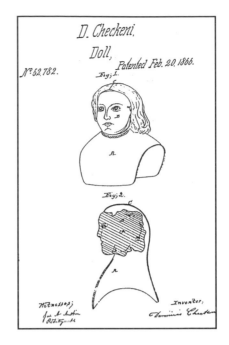

Illustration 63. Patent drawing for the 1866 Prosopotrope by Dominico Checkeni.

Illustration 64. Standing, the charming Emma L. Bristol doll (77.837), 20in (51cm) dates from the late 1890s. Emma Bristol was established in Rhode Island from 1886 to 1900, and a paper label on the front of the shoulderplate reads "Bristol's Unbreakable Doll, 273 High St. Prov. R.I." The head is made from a thick brown composition with a solid finish. Nicely detailed blue painted eyes and a crisp little mouth set close under her nose give her a piquant expression. Her brown kid body is commercially made. The smaller blonde with blue glass eyes (86.7461) is 16in (40cm) tall and is stamped on the back of the shoulderplate "Absolutely Unbreakable Patented August 2nd 1892". This patent was granted to Solomon D. Hoffmann for a composition called "Can't Break 'Em". The doll was made by the First American Doll Factory of Brooklyn, N.Y., 1892-95, which was then incorporated as the American Doll and Toy Mfg Co. until it was sold in 1908.

Illustration 65. The Webber Singing Doll (80.5035) was patented by William Augustus Webber of Medford, Mass. in 1881-83 in America as well as England, Belgium, France, Canada, and Germany. She has a wax-over composition head, large and bulging blue glass eyes, a cloth body with leather forearms, and the ability to sing her ABC's when the wooden button on her stomach is pressed, activating the music box, an example of which is shown with her. She is 22in (65cm) tall. These dolls were distributed through the Massachusetts Organ Company of Boston.

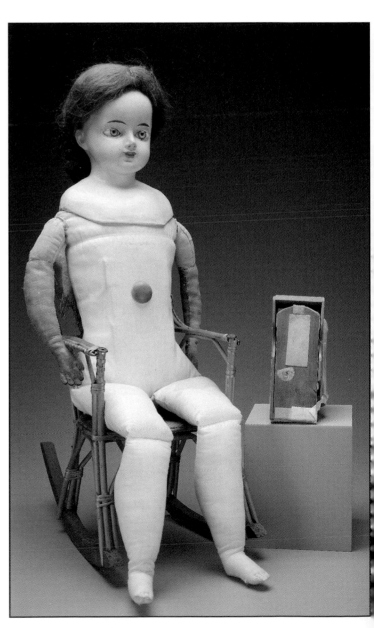

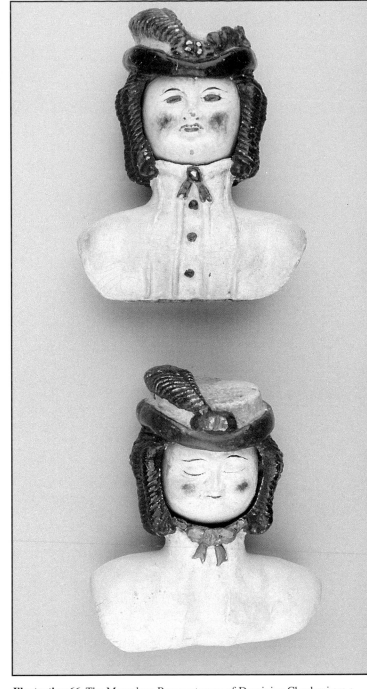

Illustration 66. The Marvelous Prosopotropes of Dominico Checkeni are a wonder to behold. They would also be fun to play with, revolving the faces on their vertical axis to reveal each of the four faces in turn. These three examples (73.1378, 73.1379, 76.892) show interesting variations. The two brightly painted heads with molded plumed hats are formed with collared blouses and squared-off shoulders. They are wax-over-composition but have been repainted. The third head, bottom right, has an obvious repair at the top; it is carved of wood which has been repainted a dark, reddish-brown. Its breastplate has deeply sloping shoulders and its revolving ball of faces is made of wax with each face having a different expression, similar to those of the hatted ladies. On all, three of the four faces have glass eyes. Patent #52,782 was issued to Dominico Checkeni of Marion, Connecticut, and noted assignment in part to George Thompson. Checkeni states in his letter to the Patent Office, "I make the bust and face of wax or any other suitable material". Labels inside the shoulderplates of the hatted ladies read: "Prosopotrope, Patented Feb. 20, 1866. Manufactured & Sold by Ozias Morse, West Acton, Mass. Sole Agent for Pantentees."

LEATHER

Leather is a marvelous material, common and exotic at the same time. Humans have tanned leather for thousands of years, employing the skills of both men and women in the process. Some Native American tribes have used leather for shelter, clothing and, of course, for dolls. The American pioneers also came to rely on leather for their personal needs. As the country became more industrialized leather was used as belts, bushings, bearings and washers, to name a few mechanical applications. Leather also became more available in finer qualities in dry goods stores, along with woven fabrics. While suitable for commercial doll bodies, leather was also used for durable, cleanable, homemade doll arms for cloth bodies. It was naturally available to every cobbler, many of whom had recently immigrated from Europe. The first time a child soaked his shoes in the rain and left them on a heater to dry, he realized that this previously pliable substance readily becomes hardened, no longer supple and comfortable. Commercial dollmakers, such as Frank Darrow of Rhode Island, and the Alkid Company recognized the potential advantage of this characteristic of leather in forming doll heads which would be firm and unbreakable. However, industrial processing left chemical residues in the leather causing paint to flake over time. In general these dolls were not as affable as the comfortable dolls of soft leather, but they attest to American ingenuity.

Illustration 67. Leather doll head 5-5/8in (14cm) (84.605) patented by Lucretia E. Sallee of Decatur Illinois in 1865 is the first doll patent registered by an American woman. The head retains its patent tag, #46,270. The patent is for construction techniques and materials aimed to produce a doll that would be safer for a child than those of breakable porcelain. The head from which the Sallee mold was made strongly resembles German china or papier-mâché heads of the period.

Illustration 68. Lucretia Sallee 1865 patent details her method of construction which involved reinforcing the inside of the leather head. After the wet leather was pressed into the head mold, a glue and plaster mixture was applied to give it a firmness yet allow it to retain its lightness. In 1873 William Brock registered a patent for a similar leather head construction but which used glue saturated fabric instead of plaster for the lining or reinforcement.

Illustration 69. Frank Darrow of Bristol, Connecticut patented and produced leather-headed dolls between 1866 and 1877. His process involved steaming the leather with a solution containing lye; this chemical process likely interacted with the paint used on the heads. These three dolls, 14 to 16 inches (35-41cm) show the classic paint conditions of Darrow dolls. From left to right, pretty badly worn woman (79.9777), an almost featureless man (79.9776), and a lady (79.9780) repainted in the 20th century.

Illustration 70. The large Alkid doll (79.10691) is just that - all kid leather and 25-1/4 inches (64.5cm). Substantial and looking much like the German bisque dolls which inspired her, she was made by the Alkid Doll Co in Portland, Oregon, 1920-21. Her coffee-colored firm body can readily challenge hard play. The company's goat trademark is stamped on the back of the torso. The other curious doll (73.1719) stands 14-1/2in (36cm) and is a late 19th century hand-made figure, very artistically proportioned and skillfully executed. It has carved wooden eyes lidded in leather and lower legs with some cloth covering, but the substantial use of leather on the head has given it inclusion in this section.

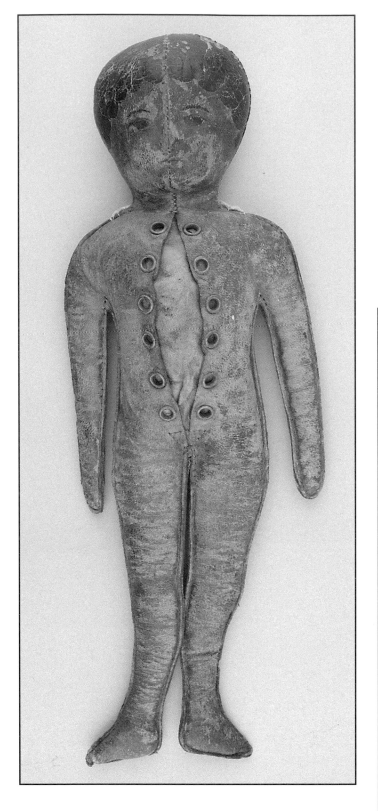

Illustration 71. The wonderful Gussie Decker doll (73.1722) with the lace-up grommetted front is distinctive and charming, 12-1/2 inches (32cm). Patented in 1903, these dolls were made by the M.S. Davis Co. of Chicago, Illinois and offered at forty cents each through Butler Bros and Sears and Roebuck, who called it baby's friend, and said the leather was "very fine to chew on when teething". In the patent description of the painted facial features and hair, Decker is not specific about the waterproof paint she recommends, but states "preferably, an indelible stain is used not affected by the action of ordinary liquids or by saliva", and advertising stated the coloring was warranted not to come off. While it was also advertised that this doll would last through several children, one can assume that parents, in the growing awareness of the relationship between cleanliness and health, might have discarded this relatively inexpensive "chewie". Others may have been confiscated by the family dog who would have found it a nicely sized and interesting toy. Wherever they went, few are known today.

Illustration 72. The 1903 patent drawing for the Gussie D. Decker leather doll (73.1722) shows its characteristic laced-up front.

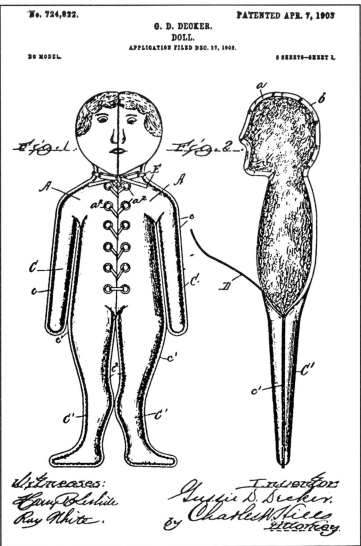

Next Page: **Illustration 73.** This group of leather dolls is but a peek at the diversity crafted through the centuries by Native Americans, peoples for whom play with dolls was an integral part of childhood. Many dolls were made for trade which also serve to document historical tribal costume. A carefully made painted leather and wood Apache cradle (77.842), from around 1910, holds a cloth doll with stitched facial features. Standing behind is the tallest, an 18-1/4in (46.5cm) high Plains doll (80.4601) with beaded sash that has a four sided cross which represents the four directions. Another Plains doll (80.4600), standing at 11in (28cm) high, with red wool leggings has white seed beads decorating her dress. Both Plains dolls date to around 1900. The warrior (80.5123) with the porcupine quill headdress was produced in 1955 through the Northern Plains Indians Craft. He is 18-1/2 in (47cm) tall. Between them is a small fringed leather play doll (83.1028) with toolwork facial features, who bears a striking resemblance to the Gussie Decker doll.

RUBBER

Liquid latex, a natural product found within many plants, is the source of rubber. It was used for centuries as a moldable material, but early rubber products were unstable to heat and cold. In l839 Charles Goodyear accidentally dropped a sulfer-rubber compound onto a hot stove. It didn't melt, but solidified and remained stable. In 1844 he obtained a patent for this process called vulcanization. This discovery facilitated the mass production of thousands of consumer products, readily created by pouring the sulphur treated liquid into heated molds. Because of personal financial problems, Goodyear licensed his discovery to other manufacturers at very low rates, became involved in infringement suits, and never saw the monetary rewards his innovative discovery might have yielded. Products created through this process included many doll types, which have great

detail but have not stood the test of time because the rubber has become brittle, warped or failed to maintain its original finish. It is rare to find a 19th century rubber-headed doll at the end of the 20th century that still has a good painted surface.

The Strong Museum is fortunate to own several fine examples. Many of the dolls and heads are shown in several pages of an 1869 catalog from the H.G. Norton & Company, found in the Strong Museum library, which are reproduced on pages 58-59. The use of rubber for dolls and novelty items continued throughout the 20th century. Almost all natural rubber comes from plantations in the Far East; during World War I rubber demands and shortages led to experiments to produce a synthetic rubber but it wasn't until the second World War that this industry exploded.

Illustration 74. Three blonde rubber-headed ladies show variances in hairstyles as well as condition. The large ladies on the ends (80.4735 and 80.4739), which are from the Goodyear Rubber Co. and date to around 1881, are almost 24 inches tall (59 and 61cm), the smaller (80.4721), from the New York Rubber Co. is 16in (41cm), and dates to around 1868. Note the sharp definition captured by a liquid substance poured into molds. Crisp facial features and hair painting are proudly retained on (80.4739). The smaller lady with the molded blouse shows typical wear and paint loss; she is pictured in the Norton catalog of 1869. All have cloth bodies with kid arms.

Illustration 75. This lady (80.4738), from the New York Rubber Co. is represented in the Norton's wholesale catalog of 1869. She has molded ringlets for her hair, and she stands 18 inches (46cm) tall with a typical cloth body with kid arms.

Illustration 76. These exquisite raven-haired sisters (83.10, 83.11) are elegant, excellent examples of rubber dolls from the New York Rubber Co. They date to around 1869. Their coral necklaces are similar to the coral necklaces seen on female children in early 19th century portraits. They are 20 and 17 inches (51 and 43cm) and have cloth bodies with kid arms.

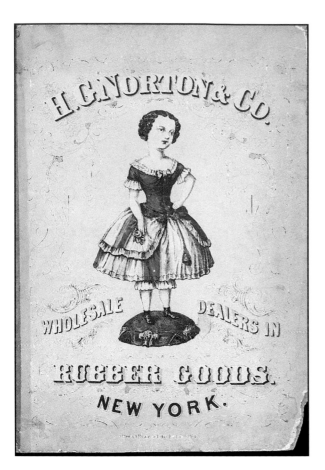

Illustration 77. The 1869 illustrated catalogue of soft and hard rubber goods manufactured for the distributor H.G. Norton & Co, New York contained many pages of dolls and toys. Many were shown in brilliant color and a price list is printed in the book. The dolls could be bought as heads or as complete dolls and a stunning variety was offered, as seen in the pages reprinted here.

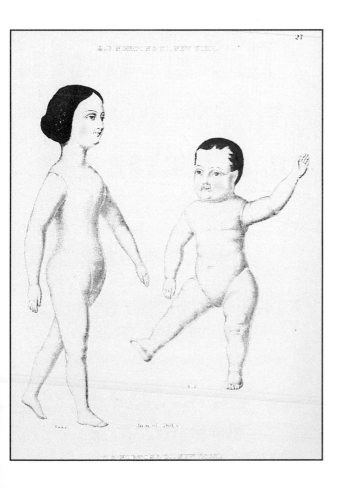

Illustration 79.
Back of blue bonnet lady (76.431)
seen in *Illustration 78.*

Illustration 78. An array of four marvelous heads and one colorful entire doll give an idea of what visual treat it would have been to see these all when new and bright. Even today, a dozen decades later, they have the ability to stop the observer's eye. Their detailed hair styles and ornamentation are dramatic and wonderful. The large blonde head (80.4708) from around 1870 to 1880, is 6in (15cm) and is marked I R Comb Co, which stands for India Rubber Comb Co., a manufacturer that produced doll heads under the Goodyear patent. The blue showing at the top of the dark haired head is the edge of a magnificient bonnet detailed in the inset. This head (76.431) is from the New York Rubber Company, stands at 3-1/2in (9cm) high, and dates from around 1869. The lady on the pedestal (80.4703), who stands at 3-1/4in (8.5cm) high and dates to around 1870, has her head turned to the side to show that her nose is extraordinarily sharp. The colorful doll with molded clothing (80.4701) was made by the New York Rubber Company around 1869. She stands at 4-1/8in (10.2cm) high. The last doll on the right (80.4723), also from the New York Rubber Company, stands at 4in (9.5cm) high, and dates to around 1868.

Illustration 80. Walt Disney's seven dwarfs (76.652) from 1938 are among the many novelty items produced throughout the 20th century in rubber. This set, made by Seiberling Latex Products Co of Akron, Ohio, comes with Snow White. Amosandra (80.4733), on the radio, is the baby from the series "Amos and Andy". A 1949 Sun Rubber Co, Barberton, Ohio doll, she was designed by Ruth E. Newton. The 10 inch (25cm) doll was patented and produced under the auspices of the Columbia Broadcasting System.

Illustration 81. Three later rubber dolls, the little girl with molded hat (80.4718) carries a tennis racquet, stands 8in (21cm) dates from the late 1890s, and was originally a squeak toy. She has no paint left, but enough charm to carry off the condition gracefully. The little brown boy (73.1480), from around 1925 and standing at 6in (15cm) high is properly attired in a molded bathing suit, as is the 1938, 8-1/2in (22cm) Charlie McCarthy (80.4710), who even has his name on a paper label on his pocket.

Illustration 82. The Deb-u-Doll, an innovative fashion plate, was designed in 1940 by Margit Nilsen, who was noted for manufacturing small-scale store window mannequins for major department stores such as Saks Fifth Avenue. The fascination these "minikins" held for both adults and children convinced her to expand her concept into the toy world. The figure's comfortable size and detachable arms facilitated a learning of sewing and fitting techniques. Deb-u-Doll is 22in (56cm); before long a 16in (41cm) Kid Sister was also made available. Both were offered with extra commercially made clothes, but often the outfits found with a Deb-u-Doll have been made from McCall patterns, at home or in a classroom, where her potential was even broader. For further information, see A. Glenn Mandeville's coverage in the October 1991 *Doll Reader®. Box and clothing courtesy of Darlene Gengelbach.*

CHINA AND BISQUE

In l8th century America, porcelain products were expensive and in limited supply. In the 19th century, European porcelain makers created imitations of Asian porcelain products, which became more affordable to consumers on both sides of the Atlantic. Once geared for large-scale manufacture, it was necessary to diversify; by the 1840s many German porcelain houses included china (glazed porcelain) doll heads and limbs in addition to their regular line of tablewares. While this production seemed a "natural" for the Germans, it was not so for Americans; American made glazed porcelain dolls are almost unknown. By World War I some porcelain dolls were made, mostly in the more popular unglazed form, called bisque.

The beginning of bisque doll manufacture in America is credited to Ernst Reinhardt, who established a pottery in East Liverpool, Ohio, in 1916. However, he encountered several difficulties in the process; his gas fired kilns were shut down due to the war effort and his excellent, made by a German immigrant, copies were boycotted because of the war. In 1918 the Fulper Pottery Co. of Flemington, New Jersey, entered the market; their financial and technical backers were among the most successful in the industry and included noted manufacturer E.I.Horsman and the Aetna Doll and Toy Co. However, the demand for, and production of, unbreakable American composition dolls was growing phenomenally fast; the days of the bisque doll were numbered.

Illustration 83. These babies and dolly-faced dolls are from the Fulper Pottery Company of Flemington, New Jersey,1918-22. Many companies used Fulper heads including Amberg and Horsman. From left to right, a 6in (15cm) shoulderhead (79.9768); a 15in (38cm) curly-topped baby on a bent-limb body (79.9769), marked "Fulper Amberg Dolls the World Standard Made in USA," and standing beside her, the only closed mouth doll (79.9771) in the group, a 17in (43cm) shoulderhead girl on a kid body with wood lower arms. Seated in front are two children, the girl (77.2338), measures 19-1/2in (49cm) high, is a shoulderhead on a kid body with bisque lower arms and hands, and is marked only: "Fulper". The 18-1/2in (47.5cm) boy (79.9770), has a jointed composition body; his head carries the Amberg mark.

Illustration 84. This wonderful and rare Fulper character (79.498) is beautifully painted, has deep blue intaglio eyes, open-closed mouth with molded upper teeth and all the charm of a Gebruder Heubach look-alike. She is 20in (50cm) tall and has a fine jointed composition body.

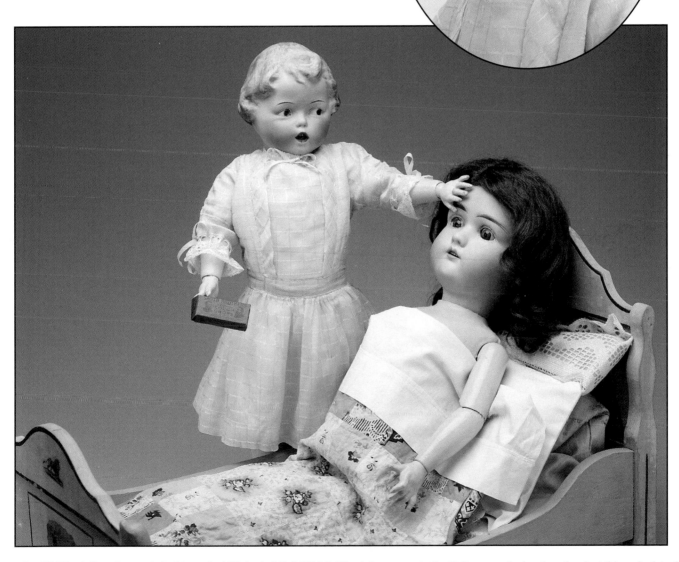

Illustration 85. The delicate beauty in bed is marked "D (script) Taft 1910 6.," but it is not certain that Taft was producing these heads at this early date. James Sholley Taft operated the Hampshire Pottery in Keene, New Hampshire, and apparently produced only a small number of dolls. Perhaps one day more details will surface. This doll is 24 inches (61cm) tall, her ears are unpierced and she apparently has caught a cold. The Fulper character attending her has a nice bed-side manner; she is offering Smith Brothers cough drops to her friend. *Taft doll from the Dorothy A. McGonagle Collection.*

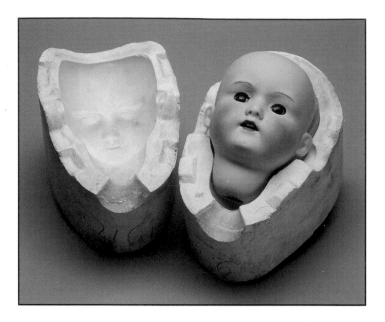

Illustration 86. *The "Augusta" bisque head (79.9660) made by Ernst Reinhardt, a German emigre, was named for his sister. Reinhardt began bisque production in East Liverpool Ohio in 1916. The 6-1/2in (16cm) head, seen in its mold, is incised on the back of the neck as: "USA / Augusta / Perth Amboy / N.J." It dates from around 1920, and it has stamped celluloid eyes. An informative research article on Reinhardt's career appears in Doll Reader®, April/May 1982 by Dorothy and Elizabeth Ann Coleman, who were instrumental in enabling the Strong Museum to obtain this mold.*

Illustration 87. This 1918 colorful china head has a molded hat marked "Liberty" (76.1852). It is 6in (15cm) tall, marked "Made in USA" on the front, and "A.P.D. Mf. Co. 122" on the back. The seated girl on a composition body (79.9783) is 20in (50cm) has blue sleep eyes and absolutely no tinting or feature painting on her face. From the Paul Revere Pottery of Boston, and dating to around 1925, these heads are often found white. The head on the bureau (79.11133) is marked "Horsman / No. 11 / Nippon". While Fulper was known to have supplied Horsman with bisque heads, this 5 inch (13cm) Nippon example, which dates from 1917 to 1930, is included here to show that American interest in bisque, though not extreme, was enough for Horsman to pursue foreign suppliers.

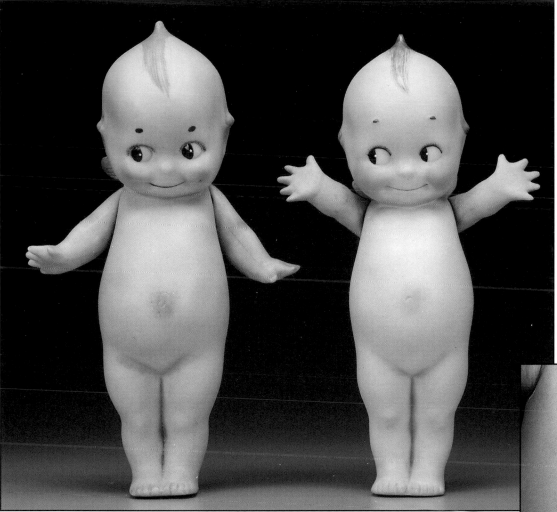

Illustration 88. Two whimsical Kewpies, designed by Rose O'Neill, 9 and 8-5/8in (23 and 22cm) tall, are both delightful scamps that date from around 1920. The one with raised arms is signed "O'Neill" on the foot and was made by Kestner of Germany (73.421) between 1912 and 1925. This 8-5/8in (22cm) doll was distributed through Borgfeldt & Co. The other (78.1035) was made by the Fulper Pottery Company between 1918 and 1921, and bears their trademark ribbon with "Made in USA" clearly incised. It is 9in (23cm) high.

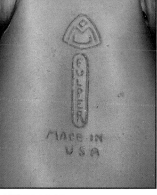

Illustration 89. Fulper mark as incised on the Kewpie to the left.

Illustration 90. Low-fired and painted bisque made from a California clay was used in the early 1940s by the Nancy Ann Story Book Doll Co of San Francisco. The smaller, bisque doll (74.209), from around 1941, stands at 5-1/2in (14cm) tall, has painted facial features and a mohair wig. Her gold wrist tag reads "To Market." The larger doll (80.5199), which stands at 6-1/2in (16cm) has a hard plastic head with painted facial features. She dates from 1946 to 1952.

CELLULOID

Celluoid was the first synthetic commercial plastic material. It was first patented in 1866 by Parkes in England because of the high demand for ivory, tortoise shell and horn which were limited in supply, high in cost and in danger of extinction. Celluloid was originally used for small personal objects such as combs but was eventually used to make an astounding variety of objects including dolls.

Unfortunately celluloid dolls had many potential aging problems including brittleness and yellowing and now have to be handled very carefully. A stronger material resembling celluloid called biscoline was developed by Parsons-Jackson and used for their dolls which can be identified by one of three registered trademarks "KKK," "Biskoline," and the drawing of a stork. The Celluoid Novelty Company of New Jersey made their dolls under the 1880-81 patents of William B.Carpenter. Louis Sametz of Westport, Connecticut, is reported to have manufactured celluloid dolls embossed with a trademarked Indian head over the word "America" as well as celluloid Kewpies marked "O'Neill".

Illustration 91. Three interesting celluloid dolls are seen here. The clockwork operated crawling baby (79.9630) is up on all fours ready to go. She measures 7-1/2in (19.3cm) to the top of her celluloid head in this position. Her body is metal, and she dates to around 1952. The anonymous football player (79.9790), from around 1940, stands 13-1/2in (34cm) and has a stuffed and sewn cloth body with marvelously exaggerated padded shoulders. The 14in (35cm) baby on the right is from the Parsons-Jackson Co (79.9899), who produced dolls from 1910-1919 of Biskoline, a celluloid-like substance they spent years developing and which they advertised could float. Note the molded and painted shoes, occasionally found on these dolls.

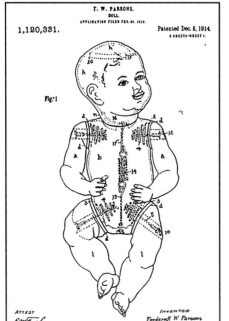

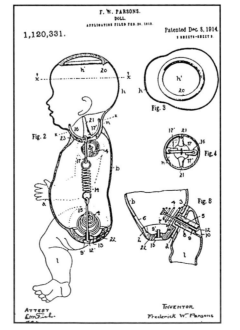

Illustration 92. Frederick William Parsons December 8, 1914 patent shows his use of metal springs for joining parts of his Biskoline baby.

METAL

Metal toys and dolls made of stamped steel, brass, aluminum and poured metal alloys became more popular during World War I due to the absence of German imports. America's heavy-duty industrialization allowed the production of even relatively trivial objects such as dolls and toys in metal. Many were copies of the German bisque heads popular at the time. Although durable, metal dolls were generally not well received by children, thus their production period was very limited. Some interesting examples can be found in the Strong Museum's collections.

Illustration 93. An eclectic array of dolls with metal heads which span nearly a half century include from left to right the 10in (25cm) "Yellow Kid" (78.11249), ca. 1900, the hero from the first colored comic sheets which were issued in 1895 by Richard F. Outcault. He has a cast metal head and a wire lever in back to move his arms. Outcault also created the popular Buster Brown and Tige characters. Beside Yellow Kid stands a 15in (38cm) tall patriotic lady (75.2611) from about 1875 wearing a liberty cap of green leaves with pink buds. The head is of cast pewter and she is on a handmade jointed wooden body with painted shoes and kid-covered upper arms. The large aluminum-headed dolly-face girl (79.9855) is from the Giebeler-Falk Doll Corp, ca. 1919. A New York City operation, they registered the trademark Gie-Fa and patented improvements to doll bodies to enable them to assume more lifelike positions. The hands and feet of this 20in (50cm) doll are also metal. The final two metal-headed babies (79.9639, 81.1052) are manually operated toys, their heads attached to wooden bellows. They show very different coloring and are 9 and 10in (23 and 25cm) tall. Each has a paper label reading: "Mama Doll I Talk 'Squeeze Me Easy' Made in America Cop. 1915 by Louis V. Aronson" and were distributed through Louis Wolf & Co. of New York City, ca 1915.

Illustration 94. Advertisement from March 1903 *Playthings* for the Metal Doll Co. of New Jersey boldly and wrongly describes their all-steel doll as the only American-made doll from the only establishment in the world where a complete doll is made!

NOVELTY

There is hardly a material known to man that someone somewhere hasn't made into a doll. Curiosities or oddities, miscellaneous novelties are delightful expressions of the creative spirit, often spontaneous in the desire to create a doll for a child. These generally employ natural materials or items that come to hand, things from bottle nipples to nuts, cornhusks to dishtowels. As 19th century magazines for homemakers flourished, so too did instructions for creating dolls, both for and as entertainment. Commercial manufacturers also created novelty items for amusement. Examples of both types from the Strong Museum collections are seen here.

Above: **Illustration 95.** Two fortune telling ladies are entertaining dolls. The composition-headed lady (80.1227) on the left is from the Sybill Fortune Telling Doll Co. of Los Angeles, ca 1925, and stands 11in (27cm) tall. The fortunes are printed on the folded papers forming the skirt. Her companion oracle (74.614), stands 10in (25cm) and from the waist up is lithographed paper on wood. Dating from about 1910, she is marked only "Patent Pending in U.S. and Abroad".

Right: **Illustration 96.** These marvelous lobster shell dolls, 12 and 16in (31 and 41cm) high, stand in testament to the variety of materials from which dolls can be made. They date to the last quarter of the 19th century. The smaller represents an old man with the walking stick (79.9280), and the other, a bagpiper (79.9277). The May 1867 *Godey's Lady's Book* contained illustrations and instructions to create these crustaceans with character; Janet Johl covers the topic in detail in *Your Dolls and Mine*. Lobster claws will never be the same again!

MECHANICAL DOLLS

The very spirit of dollmaking is to create life. Long before the products of the 19th century, men were instilling doll figures with clockwork movement. From 1850 to 1900 intricate clockwork mechanisms were being adapted by both Europeans and Americans to create some of the most beautiful and complex mechanical dolls of all time. While the French automatons were geared more toward adult entertainment, the American mechanical dolls and toys tended to have fewer movements and be more sturdily made for child's play. The clockwork gears contained within the dolls enabled the simulation of a variety of movements such as crawling or walking or even simply rolling along to amuse the child both then and now. The Strong Museum collection houses some of the finest examples ever created.

Illustration 97. Ives' Daughter of the Regiment (76.451), 9-1/2in (25cm) overall patented February 17, 1874, and dating from around 1876, stands proudly atop a drum in her uniform-like dress, blue canteen hanging from her belt and waving an American flag with eight stars. She is a clockwork-operated tin treasure.

Left: **Illustration 98.** The wonderful phonograph doll (79.9546) of Thomas A. Edison seen here dates to around 1890, though the previous decade saw Edison working on other models which did not go into production. She is 22-1/8in (56.3cm) tall. The metal torso contains the talking mechanism inscribed with numerous patent dates. An extensive article appeared in the April 26, 1890 *Scientific American Journal*, New York. The doll has a fine bisque head by Simon & Halbig of Germany, mold 719, with open mouth and teeth, through which she appears to recite a nursery rhyme which one of 18 women recorded at the Edison Toy Phonograph Co.

Above: **Illustration 99.** A walking Zouave Autoperipatetikos (76.2196) and a second one, a walking lady (76.2195), make a stunning pair. Dating from 1870, both have original boxes imprinted with "Martin & Runyan Office 289 Broadway New York". The mechanism was patented by Enoch Rice Morrison July 15, 1862 in America and noted patenting also in Europe. These heads have cloth bases, though other examples have heads of china or parian. Zouaves were French regiments originating in Algeria in 1830s; some volunteer regiments who served in both the Union and Confederate Armies during the Civil War adopted the Zouave uniform. Ladies, as noted, did their part as well.

Illustration 100. Two Ives creeping babies, one cuter than the other (76.2198 and 76.2199) have composition heads with a wax coating and clockwork mechanisms in their bodies. The mechanism was patented by Robert J. Clay on March 14, 1871. Clay owned a company called the Automatic Toy Works in New York, which was taken over by Edward Ives in 1882, who kept the best of the Clay toys in his line.

Left: **Illustration 101.** A ca. 1875 clockwork operated velocipede is ridden by an African-American boy (76.2186), whose head is the lightweight Hawkins cloth base version. His hands and lower legs are brass, his bright red coat is original. He is 8-3/4in (22.5cm) tall.

Above: **Illustration 102.** Two versions of the Old Woman in a Shoe by Ives, Blakeslee & Williams Co, ca 1890, seem ready to compete in a rolling shoe derby. Both women have wood bodies and heads with mask faces made of stamped tin. Eight little children ride in a three wheeled shoe on the left (76.2202) and three tiny china dolls in the four wheeled shoe on the right (73.1790), which also carries a label on the bottom of shoe reading: The Fair, Freund Bros Props. Detroit, Mich. Cheering them on when she gets rolling is, to the right, the Perambulating Toy (76.4015) patented December 3, 1878 by Samuel W. Adams of Boston Mass. A German china doll is raised about an inch off the platform when the pulley rotates as toy is pulled; the bent rod passing through her shoulder causes her jumping motion.

Right: **Illustration 103.** The 1878 S.W. Adams patent drawing.

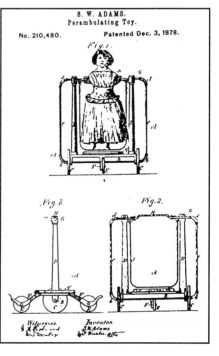

Left: **Illustration 104.** All-composition 13in (33cm) hula dancer (79.9649) operates by clockwork mechanism in her body. Made by the Zaiden Toy Works of N.Y.C. in the 1920s, she reflects an outgrowth of interest in shimmy dancing; the dolls came dressed in varied outfits. Interest in exotic Hawaii grew through the ensuing years; Hawaii became a state in 1959.

PAPER DOLLS

No one knows with certainty when or where the first paper dolls were made. An artistic hand somewhere in time cut out a drawn figure and subsequently drew costume changes. By the beginning of the 18th century, figures of this type were used in conjunction with inserted ivory miniatures to demonstrate different hair style and costumes to a client. The last quarter of the 18th century saw a commercial production of real paper play dolls which developed the name "English dolls". Paper dolls were inlaid into "toy books" such as S. and J. Fuller's "Little Henry," copied by J. Belcher, Boston, in 1812 and Philadelphia in 1825. Making paper dolls became a cottage industry in America in the 19th century. An expansion in available paper and printing in the 1830s and 1840s saw some beautiful printed, hand colored paper dolls; by the 1860s paper dolls found wider mass production. The earliest commercial American paper doll is thought to be the 1854 Chandler "Little Fanny Gray", published by Crosby, Nichols & Co. of Boston; it is of the type that is a head only

with tabs at the neck to insert into clothes. The first full-figured American commercial paper doll known is the 1857 Chandler series printed by Brown, Taggard and Chase of Boston. By the last quarter of the 19th century, giants grew out of the paper doll industry including McLoughlin Bros. of New York and Raphael Tuck who expanded from London and Paris to New York and Canada. These early paper dolls still occasionally surface, having survived being tucked away in books and linen presses for generations. Newspapers were a grand source for paper dolls which were in turn a keen advertising and selling device. A doll, given as a supplement, was provided with new and glorious weekly costumes in the newspaper, thereby hooking the collector. Fashion, theatre, movies, sports, art and history all served as inspiration for paper dolls; a microcosm of life, they are always a delight to the doll collector, student of costume or just plain child in any of us.

1850s

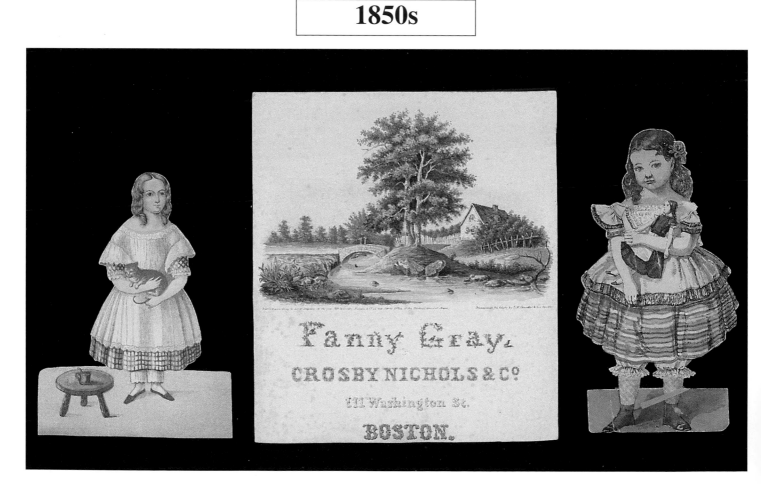

Illustration 105. "Fanny Gray" (73.438), in white pinafore and holding cat, 1854, published by Crosby, Nichols & Co., Boston, produced in oil colors by S.W. Chandler & Bros. lithographers. It is a type with head only and separate costumes. Insert shows cottage background scenes where Fanny lived. "Susie's Pets", 1858, (73.439) early McLoughlin Bros with front and back clothing, striped skirt, holding a doll.

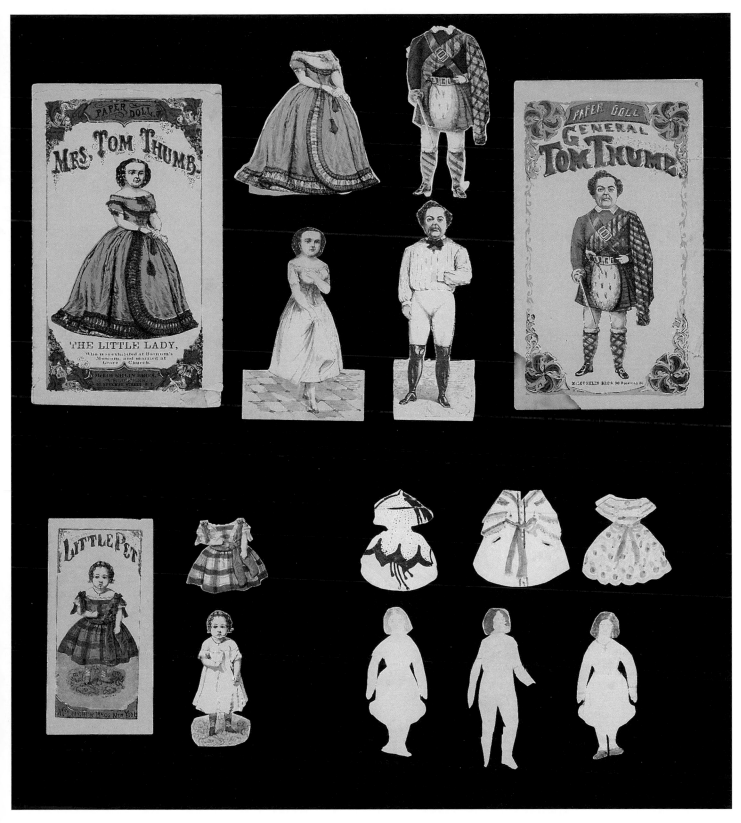

Illustration 106. *Top Row:* Mrs. Tom Thumb (77.2574) and her General, ca 1864, McLoughlin Bros, New York, lithographed and hand colored, They have several dresses and the uniforms worn before Emperor Louis Napoleon and Empress Eugenie. Mrs. Thumb outlived Tom by 36 years, and died at age 78 in 1919. *Bottom row, left:* "Little Pet" (77.2587), ca 1865, Series No 1; one doll and one dress shown, McLoughlin Bros. (Right) Handmade set (77.277) includes three figures, three extra dresses and provenance; it was made by Tillie Campbell in 1868 at age 10 for her sister Ursulla in Geneva, New York.

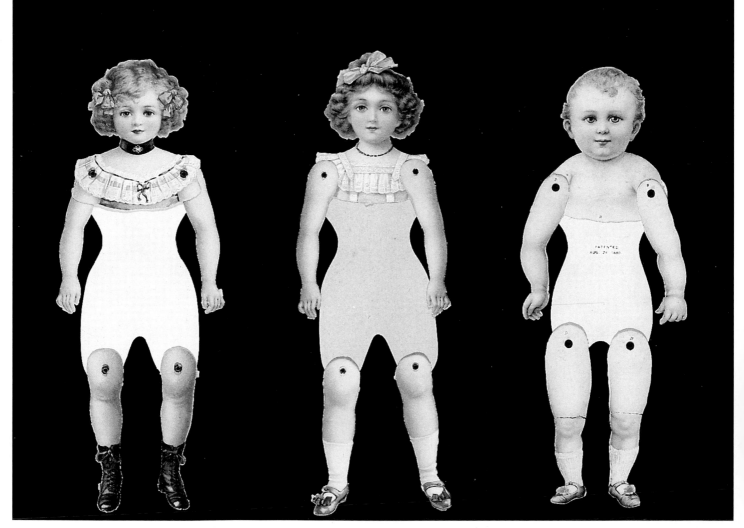

Illustration 107. *Top Row:* "Little Dolly Varden" (77.2604), ca 1875, McLoughlin Bros. She was a character from Dicken's Barnaby Rudge. From same series, McLoughlin's Clara Louise Kellog (77.2609), American operatic soprano, dates to around 1875. *Bottom Row:* Three Dennison Mfg. Co, N.Y. children, from left to right (78.2592, 89.4684, 78.2758), activated by rivet joints, printed in Germany by Littauer & Bauer around 1880.

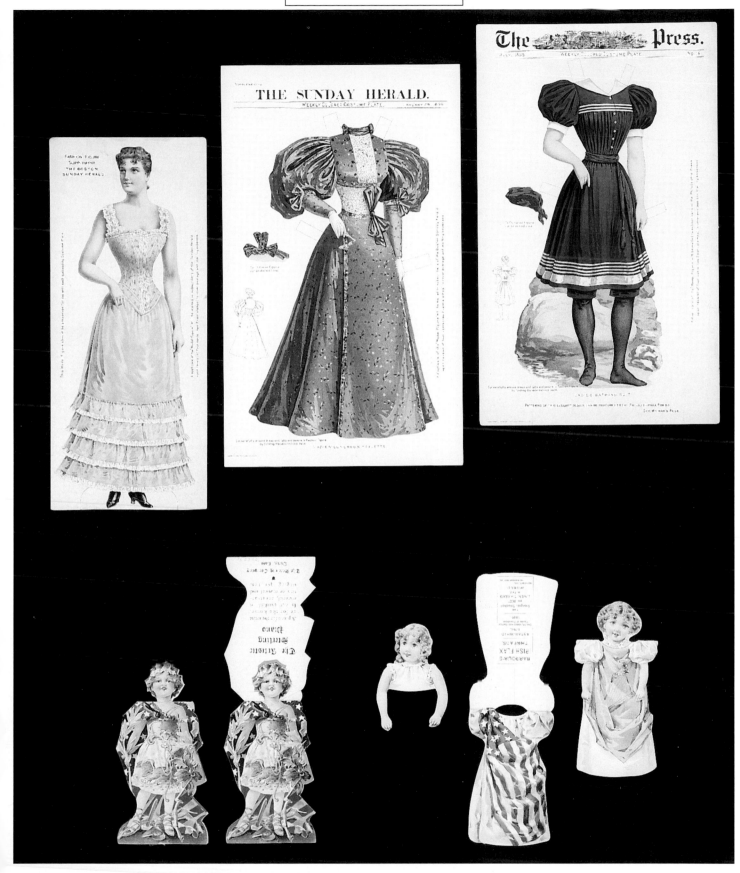

Illustration 108. *Top Row:* *The Boston Sunday Herald* blonde lady, the "Model Figure" (75.2362), 1895, G.H.Buck & Co, lithographer, also given as supplement in other newspapers including *Philadelphia Press*. Costume plates printed weekly; shown are green luncheon toilette (75.2352) and bathing suit (75.2218). *Bottom Row:* Patriotic advertising, The Sterling Company's Artistic Piano enticement shows flag-draped girl (77.6231, 77.6232), early 1900s, with symbolic touches in wheat, apples and ax. Next to her is a flag-draped girl (77.5756.1, .2) advertising for Barbour Bros. Irish Flax Threads, which dates to ca. 1895.

Illustration 109. The Lettie Lane paper family, *Presenting Lettie's Baby Sister with Her Nurse and Some of Her Belongings* (75.2747), drawn by Sheila Young, 1909, Curtis Publishing Co., Philadelphia, PA.

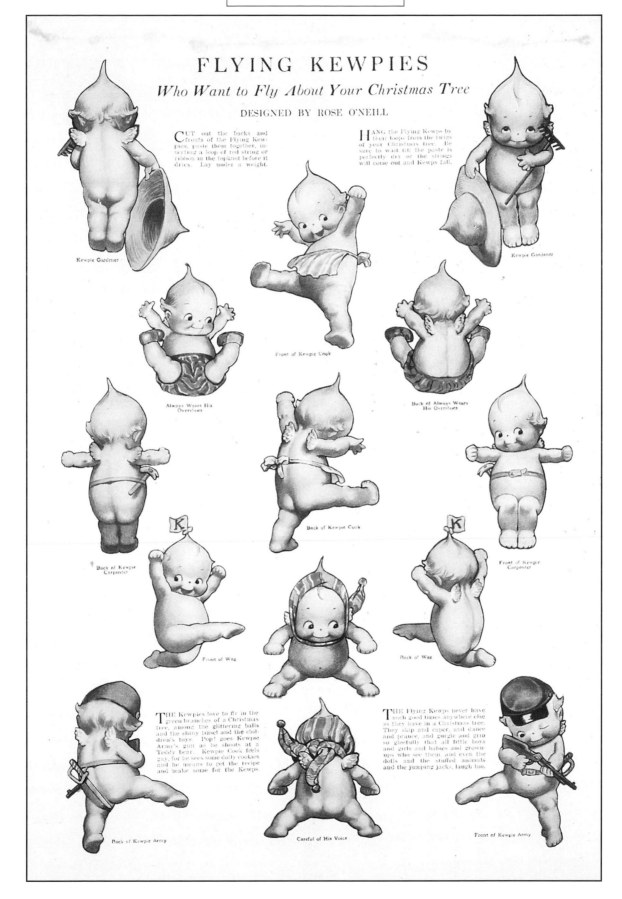

Illustration 110. Rose O'Neill's *FLYING KEWPIES Who Want to Fly About Your Christmas Tree* (77.191), 1914. The Crowell Publishing Co, New York. Front and back Kewpies designed to be cut out and pasted together as tree ornaments.

Illustration 111.

Right: Gaylord-Alderman Company's clever 1920 advertising paper doll (86.7768) wears dresses available from their store as she demonstrates her patriotic efforts: junior auxiliary, knitting socks, holding a book of thrift stamps and a U.S. airplane, and displaying a window flag denoting that a family member is in the service of our country.

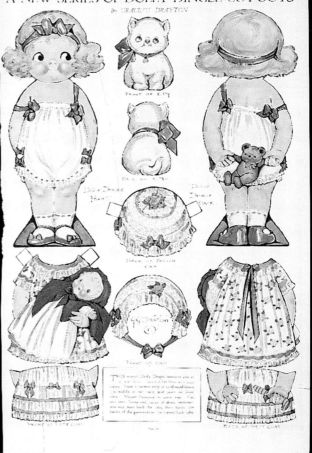

Illustration 112. *Bottom Row:* The popular impish children of Grace G. Drayton that appeared in the Pictorial Review Co, New York. "Sammy Gets Ready for the Baseball Season" (76.2940) is from 1920, and the girl with back and front views (86.3034) dates to 1919.

Illustration 113. *Top Row:* The Hollywood Dollies Inc, New York, 1925, a "Series of Life-Like Miniatures of Famous Motion Picture Stars in Original Costumes Worn in Pictures" included Tom Mix (75.2387) and Norma Talmadge (75.2389). *Bottom Row:* Paper dolls include Queen Holden's 1930 "Gloria" lovingly holding her doll (76.1120) from Whitman Publishing Co.; the Shirley Temple paper doll (76.3763) with costumes from her movies, 1938, Saalfield Publishing; Walt Disney's Snow White and the Seven Dwarfs, (76.3817) from Whitman Publishing, 1938; and the 1940 MGM classic Gone With the Wind, (76.3746) featuring Clark Gable and Vivien Leigh, from Merrill Publishing Co, Chicago.

Illustration 114. The 1940s were dominated by "World War II; Air, Land and Sea Paper Dolls" (76.3758), 1943, Van Sweringen, Saalfield Publishing, featured 3 men and 3 women in all branches of service.

1950s

1960s

Illustration 115. *Top Row:* the 1950s homemaking interests encouraged young girls toward wedding thoughts in play, "Bridal Party Cut-out Dolls", (94.4143) drawn by Hilda Miloche, Whitman Publishing Co, 1950. Annie Oakley (76.3950) of television and motion pictures demonstrates nostalgia for the good old days, Whitman Publishing, 1954. Grace Kelly (94.1092), MGM Star was an American "princess" before she became a real one, Whitman Publishing, 1955, and Elizabeth Taylor (94.1093), who grew from beautiful child star to beautiful woman while a country watched, remained a fascination, Whitman Publishing, 1956. *Bottom Row:* "The John F. Kennedy and His Family", (95.29) created by Tom Tierney in 1990 for Dover Publications, Inc. reflects Kennedy's time in office; Twiggy, (77.5822) the English mod fashion figure in an authorized edition by Western Publishing Co, Racine, WI, 1967; Barbie® and Ken® (77.5830), licensed by Mattel, Whitman Publishing Co, 1962, who followed closely on the popularity of the fashion plate dolls with myriad interests and clothes to match; Walt Disney's 1961 Annette in Hawaii (76.3820), Whitman Publishing Co, shows Mousketeer Annette Funicello's continued popularity.

Illustration 116. Paper dolls through the last decades of the 20th century continued to draw on the field of entertainment, and included notable figures from all walks of life, current as well as retrospective works. The bell-bottomed Brady Bunch (94.1091), 1972, all-American family seen in Western Publishing Co's press-out dolls and wardrobe set. Two recent series, "Famous African-American Women" (95.30) and "Bill Clinton and His Family" (95.31), Dover Publications, Inc, 1994, are by the very talented Tom Tierney and show his interest in notable historical figures and today's celebrities, recording history as it happens.

CLOTH

Soft and warm, limp and cuddly, folky and funky are all images that come to mind when hearing the term "Rag Doll". Often these dolls were born of the rag bag by loving mothers, painted with natural dyes and inks, or stitched by hands with varying levels of skill. Yet almost invariably they were the most played with and loved, and were the most comforting dolls to take to bed, even if the non-cloth variety was considered more special at play time. These are the dolls of America that inspired the creations of inventive women in their later mercantile cloth doll production. The vast majority of commercially produced cloth dolls grew from the hands and hearts of women like Izannah Walker, Martha Chase, Emma

Adams, Julia Beecher and their contemporaries, who wanted children to have dolls that would not harm them if dropped and broken; dolls that felt good to hold and that nurtured domestic qualities. These concerns and successes were continued during the 20th century, as evidenced by the numerous representations from the Strong Museum collection in three basic areas: Primitive or Folk Art, Home Industry and Manufactured cloth dolls.

PRIMITIVE OR FOLK ART

ONE-OF-A-KIND,
FEW-OF-A-KIND,
INSPIRED,
ENDEARING,
CLOTH DOLLS

Illustration 117. Many Native American dolls were made for the souvenir trade. The tall doll (80.5126) is all cloth with skillfully painted facial features. It stands 17in (43cm) and is marked with the following inscription, "Head painted / by Helen Allen Ettrick Wisc. / Body & Clothes Made by / Hattie S. McLaud at RD2 Canastota, N.Y., 1942 / Shoes from Reno." A Cheyenne native, from Fort Sill in Oklahoma, made the other two, 13in (33cm) high, Plains dolls (76.811, 76.812), which date from around 1938.

Illustration 118. These are among the earliest cloth dolls in the Strong Museum collection. On the left, a tiny handmade cloth doll wearing a white cotton dress with lavender print rests inside an arch-shaped box (80.1633) lined with cut out paper flowers and leaves. On the box back is inscribed a partially legible provenance, "Presented — by Her— Hannah in the Fall of 1839 Made by —R.I." She is just over 4in (10cm) tall. The larger doll (74.194), 8in (21cm) is perhaps even older; the early 19th century is suggested by her sloped shoulders and sleeves. She is carved wood covered with cloth, her penciled features barely distinguishable. Her blue apron was carefully pinked and edged by hand.

Illustration 119. There were two old women who lived in shoes... Both depicting the nursery rhyme, the blue satin shoe on the left (79.9976) dates from 1860 and has 15 small cloth dolls or heads sewn into the shoe, some not visible. Each head has painted features and each doll marvelously detailed clothing. The overall length of the shoe is only 4in (19cm). Slightly larger accommodations were needed for the 1870 family who live in a 6in (15cm) shoe (73.1735), also with 15 occupants. As these dolls are larger, there is greater overcrowding in this shoe; two tiny heads protrude from the toe. Written on the sole of the shoe is "Nursery Rhyme of the Old Woman in Shoe."

Illustration 120. Knitted and crocheted dolls have a beloved ancestry. This beautiful Quaker couple (80.1668) have been together since at least the 1890s. In their scant 8in (20cm) size, they are handsomely detailed, she with her poke bonnet and umbrella and he with his handsome felt hat, wing collar, black suit and walking stick. The larger patriotic young lady (78.3149) is 9-1/2in (24.5cm) and is the type of doll that appeared as patterns in various women's periodicals such as *Harper's*, though they were also offered commercially by distributors who recognized their great appeal.

Illustration 121. In contrast to the four simple dolls, this marvelous African-American woman (79.9941) is a sophisticated creation. Other dolls with the same modeling, open-closed mouth with painted teeth and startling blue eyes have been found in the Lancaster, Pennsylvania area. She is 17in (43cm) tall, has holes in her ears and nostrils, and a wig of black lamb's wool. Her well-made brown cloth body is stuffed with cork, and her mitt hands show a well defined thumb and fingers delineated by stitches.

Illustration 122. Four African-American folk art dolls from the first quarter of the 20th century display a broad charm within varying levels of difficulty of construction. Each is unique, has embroidered features, and wears clothing that is competently sewn, suggesting the makers were skilled with a needle. The tall doll (80.1732), 19in (48cm), has a gentle face, button eyes, red embroidered mouth and a fur wig that has startlingly faded with time. In front of her are, left, a 13-3/4in (35.5cm) man (79.9985) of black sateen with white cloth eyes sewn on with black thread, red thread mouth and cloth covered cardboard nose. He wears a wonderful checked wool swallow-tail suit with a jaunty red tie. In the center, 14-1/2in (37cm) Sarah (87.1584), who has much more nose than she shows, wears a lovely white dress and comes with a bit of her history. She was handmade in 1910 by a Rochester, New York woman. On the right, another Rochester woman, Gertrude Bassett, made the 15in (38cm) button-eyed boy (87.1643), circa 1925.

Illustration 123. This wonderful little turn of the century family (80.1745), dressed in their Sunday best. The mother is only 10in (25cm) tall, the smallest child a mere 2-1/2in (6cm). All are constructed of the same stockinet over wire, but the mother has had a kid covering added over her head onto which her bright eyes and mouth are painted and a kid nose applied. The children have painted features and all have string hair.

Illustration 124. These five handmade cloth dolls all have painted features and probably were made within a 20 year period. In the back, the large 29in (74cm) ca 1890 apple-cheeked primitive lady (79.9981) with very dark hair retains vivid oil coloring. Skillfully drawn and painted, her patrician nose, clear blue eyes and demure smile give her a kindly authority. A drawing of the fabric into the seam around her head gives a sense of texture to her hair. Her body is well-proportioned with fingers separate. The large doll to her right (79.9962) is from around 1890, has a well-made body with separately attached thumb, a nice detail. Somewhat thick of neck, she has a back center seam that forms a pointed bun with a painted pink bow. She may be one of two dolls from the same family as a very similar doll with a blue hair bow was noted in a private collection. In the center, a 22in (55cm) 5-piece cloth head with a simple hand-painted face (85.949) is sewn to a cloth body with kid arms of the type manufactured by Charles F. Braitling in the late 19th century. The head is attributed to Sarah Garrison Huff in 1910. The whimsical Humpty Dumpty face (85.998) is ink drawn on a man's stiff collar, likely from a woman's magazine pattern, early 20th century. The final doll (80.1742) is also probably made from a professional pattern, ca 1880s. Made of muslin, she has mitt-type hands with a separate thumb and feet sewn and painted as slippers. She has a center part hairstyle with three spitcurls onto her temples.

Illustration 125. These three dolls were obviously made from the same pattern and more than likely the same hand. The two in front, Lollipop and Henry, came from Rhode Island and Massachusetts, and are more identical in hair style, having two curls and a smooth hairline. At 16-1/2in (42cm) they are nearly an inch bigger than the Strong Museum's ca. 1885 doll (80.1742), but these differences are minor. Lollipop and Henry from the *Dorothy A. McGonagle Collection.*

Illustration 126. This 21-1/2in (54cm) lady (79.9939) with the rather refined demeanor is quite wonderful. She has an oil painted face, with a center seam that gives her added character. Her long blonde flowing hair is of cotton crochet thread stitched into the head; the front hair is drawn back into a braid and exposes her nicely ruffled ears. She dates from about 1875. The seven tiny rolled cloth dolls residing in and on her bureau (79.9977, 79.9978, 79.9971, 79.9972, 79.9973, 79.9974) have delicate embroidered features, range in size from 3 to 6in (7.5-15cm) and their exquisite costumes are in remarkably good scale. Several have human hair wigs. Note the infant (79.9935) on the left atop the bureau; she was formed on a wishbone. All are ca. 1881.

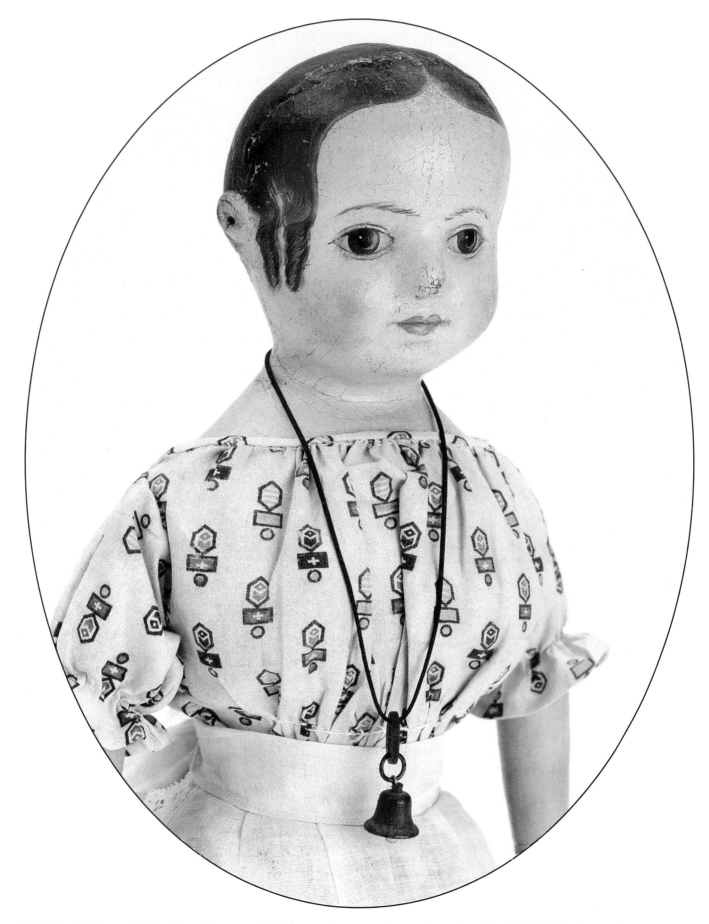

Illustration 127. Izannah Walker, the quintessence of 19th century oil on canvas became three-dimensional doll. This lovely example measures 18in (45.5cm) high, and her painting reflects the style and finish of dolls prior to the 1873 patent.

IZANNAH WALKER

The essence of a letter written by her grand-niece, a Mrs. Norman Robertson, describes Izannah Walker of Central Falls, Rhode Island as an artist, dollmaker, inventor, canary raiser, dabbler in real estate, and one who heard voices in the night, and acted on them... Some might have called her eccentric, but the voice telling her to use paste in the final process of pressing two shells of one head together in the set of dies must have spoken earlier, suggesting that she pad the two shells with cotton batting; for it is that padded layer that gives her heads a certain tenderness to touch. This is the fiber of her 1873 patent; the legacy she left came from a gifted hand, a soul and a spirit that enriched not only 19th century American life, but today's.

Illustration 128. A flock of Walkers can take one's breath away. From left to right are seen a 17-1/2in (45cm) Izannah Walker in a blue dress (79.9929), who reflects a style of modeling found on examples with the head made as a separate part and attached to the torso, c. 1880. Handwritten in black ink on the inside rim of this doll's shoulderplate is: Patented Nov. 4th, 1873. The other dolls are more consistent with earlier painting; they included a 20in (51cm) girl (79.9927) with two curls in front of her ears, similar to the 18in (45.5cm) girl with the bell around her neck (73.1478). The barefoot Izannah Walker (76.810) seated on the chair is only 13-3/4in (35cm) while the doll on the far right (79.9926) stands 18-1/2in (47cm). Izannah Walker dolls saw many years of production prior to their patenting, thereby making precise dating difficult. However, enjoyment of their grace and style is easy.

Illustration 129. Carl Wiegand patent model heads, #177,777 dated May 23, 1876, unpainted and painted, 4in (10cm) (84.606). The Wiegand patent details the construction process: in the molding, a layer of paper and glue is sandwiched between two layers of fabric.

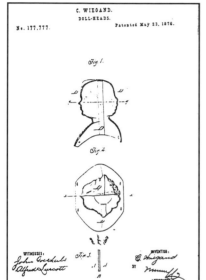

Illustration 130. Carl Wiegand 1876 patent drawing.

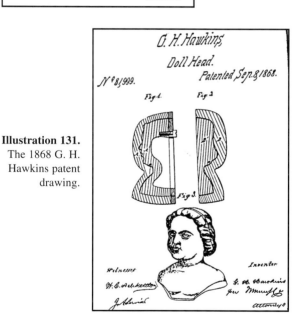

Illustration 131. The 1868 G. H. Hawkins patent drawing.

Illustration 132. Three cloth-headed dolls from different manufacturers include the tall blonde (85.4653), 28in (72cm) who bears the label reading "Wiegand's Patent Head, May 23rd, 1876." She has blue painted eyes and delicately colored and outlined mouth. The dark-haired lady (79.9938) has a linen head with a wire around the rim of the shoulderplate which is covered with a thick coat of paint. Collectors refer to them as "mystery" linen heads, because their maker is unknown. She measures 23in (59cm), has pupil-less black painted eyes, feathered brows, red lip coloring, and dates to around 1860. The lady pushing the carriage (76.2192) has a head made under the 1869 patent of George H. Hawkins which described his method of pressing fabric saturated with glue or size between dies until it hardened. These heads are often found on mechanical toys such as this from Wm. F. Goodwin, 1875, and as seen on page 71, though occasionally also on a typical doll's body.

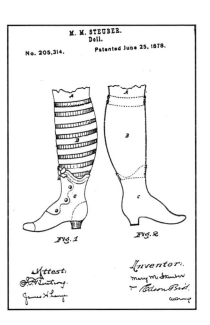

Illustration 133. The 1878 M. M. Steuber patent is for her characteristic booted foot.

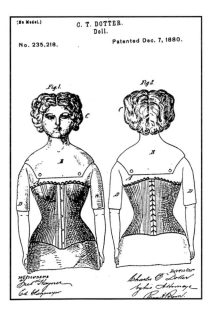

Illustration 134. The 1880 C. T. Dotter patent shows a corset as part of the body construction.

Illustration 135. Printed cloth bodies were a serious manufacture. They were sold to assemblers to use with imported heads or alone to replace worn out bodies, and were a standard offering through Butler Bros. What an eye-catching idea, these brightly colored printed bodies combining education and entertainment. These dolls are often imprinted with the alphabet, animals, or arithmetic problems, like this 11-1/2in (29cm), ca. 1910 doll (73.403). During the Spanish-American war patriotic symbols were popular, as exemplified by this 16in (41cm), ca. 1900 doll (76.894). Note the map detailing the pertinent American conquests — San Juan, Puerto Rico, Manila, etc. Another, from around 1910, shows flags of all nations (73.404) on its 9-1/2in (24cm) tall body, and on the ca. 1895, 11in (28cm) doll the American Eagle seal (78.357) is proudly emblazoned along with the names of the states. They have become significant trinkets.

Martha Wellington

Martha L. Wellington of Brookline, Massachusetts was granted a patent on September 25, 1883, for an improvement in the construction of stockinet dolls. She specified the use of a "wire frame bent into the contour of the head, face and neck" which was stuffed with cotton batting and covered with flesh colored tubular stockinet. Oil colors were preferred for painting the dolls' face, arms and lower legs. The fingers were curled with the thumbs separate. Her distinctive baby dolls are rarely found, but sometimes have her patent dates (January 8, 1883, September 25, 1883) stamped on the bodies.

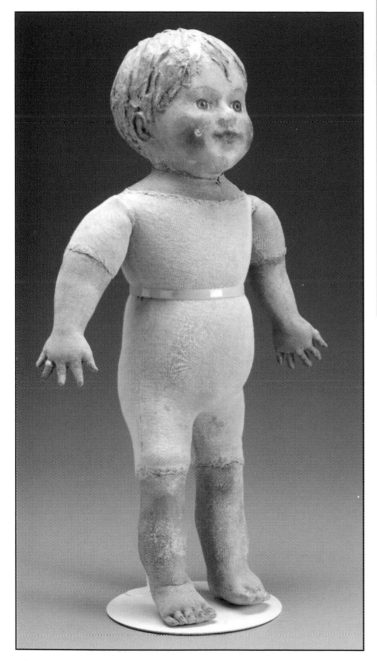

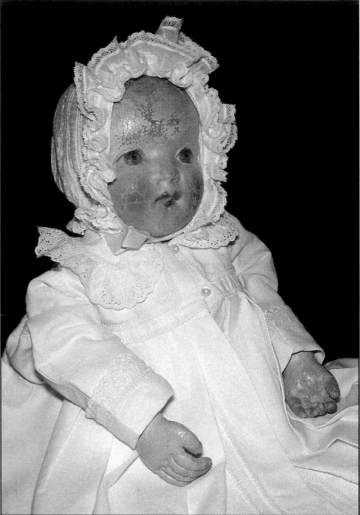

Illustration 136. This treasured baby shows all the realistic charm that Martha Wellington intended to convey in her babies. The molded eyelids are classic Wellington, and the subtly multi-colored eye painting enthralling, ca. 1885, 23in (58.5cm). There are different looks to Wellington babies; any could be lived with, but this is definitely one of the prettiest. Not seen are her dimpled feet and another Wellington trademark, a well-shaped and padded baby bottom. She is 23in (59cm). *Marilyn Johnson Collection. Photo by Dorothy McGonagle.*

Illustration 138. Martha L. Wellington's 1883 patent shows the wire frame bent to form the contour of the head.

Illustration 137. This distinctive molded stockinet doll (79.9963) has a muslin covered face which is confidently painted. The stockinet lower limbs are also stiffened and painted, but it is the uniquely textured hair treatment, an applied papier-mâché, that is so individual. The eyes are beautifully painted with two almost impressionistic white highlights in each eye giving them great dimension. He stands almost 20in (49cm). These dolls have recently been attributed to Dorothy Klinghorn Wilson, c. 1910.

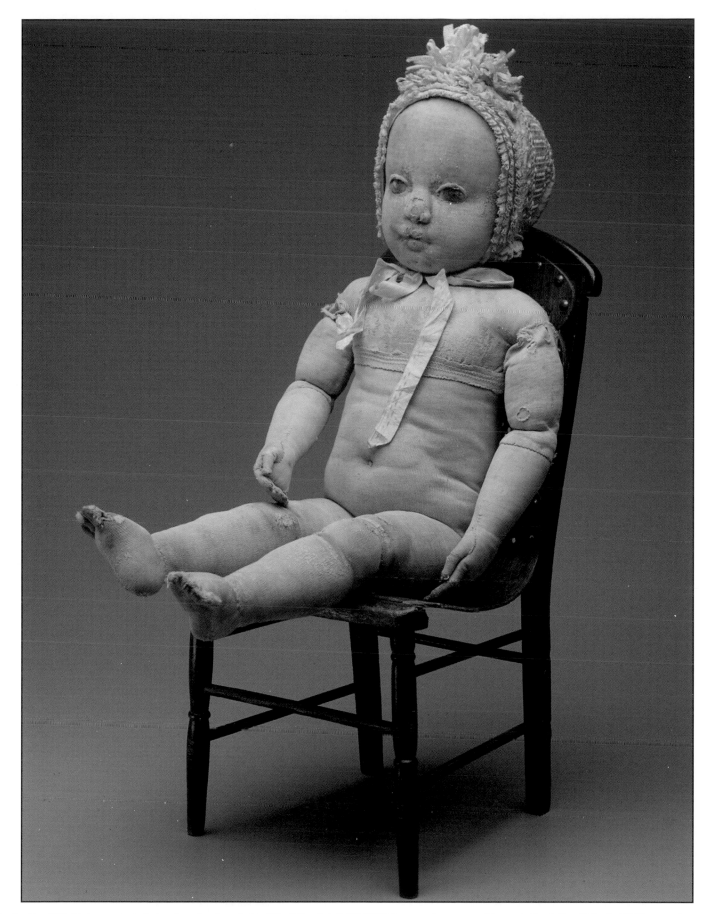

Illustration 139. Unknown but obviously not unloved, this 25in (64cm) doll (79.9969) bears a strong resemblance to the dolls of Martha Wellington. A comparison, however, shows construction differences, making positive attribution impossible, although marked examples also show variations. The fingers of this baby are not as cupped as traditionally found on a Wellington, but that may have evolved through the years. The molded eyelids, though, are very similarly formed and the facial expression indicates Wellington bloodlines. The only mark on this doll is an inked 83 on the fabric of the left forearm; while it is a nice coincidence that 1883 is the year of the Wellington patent, the mark could conceivably be part of the fabric manufacturer's coding.

PRINTED CLOTH DOLLS

The development of inexpensive printing techniques encouraged a profusion of dolls printed on fabric from the mid 1880s onward. Some were sold by the yard to be assembled at home, others were already made up. Many were simply front and back pieces while others, like the Ida Gutsell products, required more skill to piece together. Numerous design patents were granted for printed dolls; Edward Peck's in 1886 for a Santa Claus figure is considered the first. The textile-producing area of the Northeast was also the site of many of the printing houses, including the Art Fabric Mills of Cocheco, New York and the Arnold Print Works of Massachusetts, for whom Celia and Charity Smith designed some of the first by-the-yard dolls. By the 20th century many were produced as advertising dolls, inexpensively or in exchange for box tops, a highly successful endeavor that continues in various forms today.

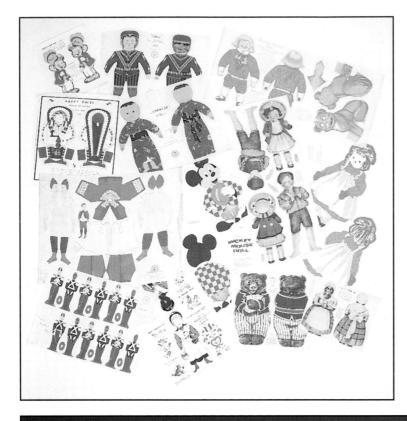

Illustration 140. A mosaic of uncut cloth dolls spanning nearly a century includes several familiar advertising faces. Clockwise from the bottom left, "Our Soldier Boys" (75.5121), 1892; Ida Gutsell's boy in blue (78.391), 1893; "Happy Chief" (75.5131), 1970; "Kellog's Pop" (75.5145), 1948; "Columbian Sailor Doll 1492" (78.359), 1893; "Buster Brown & Tige" (78.392), 1915; "Raggedy Ann" (76.1780), 1960s; "Mammy Castoria" (76.1750), 1950; "Kellog's Daddy Bear" (75.5119), 1926; "Mine Nawma Iss Becky" (75.5139), 1970; Walt Disney' Mickey Mouse Doll (75.5114), 1937; Betsy and Bill Permanent Dolls (76.1756), 1913; and a charming Japanese Doll (75.5123), 1893.

Illustration 141. A group of Brownies designed by Palmer Cox for the Arnold Print Works, North Adams, Mass, 1892 includes the uncut framed Uncle Sam and five made up figures (74.1481, 74.609, 74.611, 74.612, 73.1764, 74.1469). The Brownies originated in 1887; these imaginary mischievous good fellows appeared in Cox's stories, setting things right while others slept; their popularity was and remains legendary. The Brownie face became synonymous with Eastman Kodak's inexpensive Brownie Box Camera, introduced in 1900, which made photography available to nearly everyone.

Illustration 142. Cut and stuffed, this colorful group of printed cloth dolls includes the 1886 Edward Peck Santa Claus (74.196), 15in (38cm), surrounded by, left to right, a 16in (40.6cm) Little Red Riding Hood (74.195), inscribed on base "Patented July 5, 1892 & Oct. 4, 1892 Arnold Print Works"; a 24in (62cm) Miss Flaked Rice (79.9964), from the American Rice Foods Mfg.Co., 1899; a 19-1/2in (49cm) George Washington (76.1856), Art Fabric Mills, 1901, and a 15-1/2in (39cm) Ida Gutsell boy doll (76.9934) from Cocheco Mfg Co, 1893, who was well sewn. Note his decided chin and removable clothing, a feature of her design. An informative article on printed cloth advertising dolls by Donna C. Kaonis appeared in the Sept/Oct 1994 *Inside Collector*.

Illustration 143. Three topsy-turvy dolls, each with a Caucasian face and an African-American face include, clockwise from upper right, an 11in (28cm) by Albert Bruckner (73.1753), patented July 8, 1901 and distributed by Horsman. The colorfully dressed and well-hatted doll (81.1111) is unmarked, 10in (26cm) and is also from the turn of the century. The third (81.1113) bears a stamp on the Caucasian face, "Patent No. 185188", and measures 11in (28cm).

Illustration 144. The Mother's Congress Doll Co. of Philadelphia manufactured printed cloth dolls from the Nov 6, 1900 patent granted Madge Lansing Mead (79.9966). A unique feature of the seven piece pattern was that the head was made from a single piece. The name Baby Stuart is often found stamped on these dolls. Few have survived in excellent condition. This doll needs cleaning, a chore being attempted by Goldie and Dusty, the 5-1/2in (14cm) Gold Dust twins (81.653 & 81.654), premium representatives of the Fairbanks Gold Dust Washing Powder Co, and made by the Nelke Corporation ca. 1925.

Next Page: **Illustration 145.** A large Columbian Doll (79.9982), 29in (74cm) with rosy cheeks and beautiful blue eyes, painted by Emma Adams, late 1890s, sits with a cloth doll, the bonnetted charmer, which she surely inspired. This doll was called a Babyland Rag Doll (79.9967), produced by Horsman, and released in 1904. Many sizes were offered, these 14in (36cm) were among the most popular. The Babyland Rag with the lithographed face (73.1725) is "Automobile Girl" ca. 1910.

THE COLUMBIAN DOLL OF EMMA ADAMS

Even undressed, a doll painted by Emma Adams has a certain completeness and appeal. Competently sewn and confidently painted, these charmers were called the "Columbian Doll" after Emma was awarded a Diploma of Honorable Mention at the 1893 Columbian Exposition in Chicago, where they captivated fairgoers. Assisted by her family, especially her sister Marietta who designed the clothing, Emma and her doll saw great success. When Emma died suddenly as a young woman in 1900, her sister continued the production; the later dolls are stamped: Manufactured by Marietta Adams Ruttan. The Emma rosebud mouth, outlined nose and lustrous eyes were emulated by others, including the artists who continued her work under Marietta's care, but the magical qualities of Emma Adams' art were unique.

BEECHER BABY

Illustration 146. Julia Beecher's 24-1/2in (62cm) needle sculpted silk jersey Missionary Ragbabies (78.358) were successful fundraisers for the Park Congregational Church in Elmira NY, from 1893 to 1910. Hand painted, sewn features and yarn hair distinguish them. Note ear detail in inset. Additional information is found on page 21 about dolls made as fundraisers by churchwomen.

MARTHA JENKS CHASE

Martha Jenks Chase of Pawtucket, Rhode Island is recorded as sewing a doll for her daughter, Bessie, in 1876 as a Christmas gift. It is also known she played with an Izannah Walker doll as a child. A remarkable woman, the daughter and wife of physicians and influenced by a socially concerned mother, she was staunchly involved in the Progressive movement of the time. Martha Chase took a practical rather than a simply intellectual path, practicing what she preached. She started her business in 1891 in a small outbuilding in her back yard. She later hired needy and underprivileged girls and women to help her in what was fondly called the "dolls' house". Her soft-featured dolls had great practical and artistic appeal, and her advertising stressed that the dolls "could be washed with warm water keeping infecting germs from our babies." Made of fine stockinet, the faces were formed by pressing sized material into a mold. When dry, the mask was attached to a firmly packed ball mounted on a stick. The back of the head was attached with stitches similar to those on a baseball. The doll's body was made of heavy white cotton cloth, with stockinet stretched over it. Every part was firmly packed with stuffing including the fingers which are separated, with the thumb attached as a separate piece. The ears are also separately attached. The completed dolls were sized again to facilitate shaping the fingers and toes, and a coat of paste was applied before the doll was finished with oil paints. The paint for the hair was thickly applied with a coarser brush to give texture. Chase dolls are not wigged because Martha Chase wanted them to be cleanable. Earlier dolls had sateen covered bodies, but later ones are completely painted, rendering them washable. Many of her dolls were used in hospitals to train nurses; these included both weighted baby (7 lbs) and adult size mannikins, made with the same techniques as the play dolls. The Strong Museum has a large collection of her works, including the notable George Washington portrait seen on the cover, literary characters and numerous children for child's play. Martha Chase died in 1925 but her family continued the business until 1978, primarily manufacturing teaching dolls for hospitals, although play dolls of vinyl were also made in the company's last years.

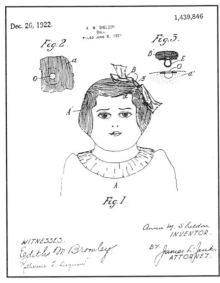

Illustration 147. The 1921 patent registered by Martha Chase's daughter, Anna Margaret Sheldon, for a snap-on hairbow.

Illustration 148. A group of blonde Chase children show several variations in body and hair styles. On the left is an undressed girl (81.393) with an all-painted "hospital" body which has no joints in the limbs and which could be completely washed, 1920-1930. She has a wonderful side part in her deeply modeled hair and stands 16in (41cm) as does the dressed boy (81.387) beside her, who also has a side part plus a curl. The smaller dressed boy (77.2877) is 13in (33cm) and has an open mouth. The seated girl in front (81.389) has unusual side-jointed limbs; the arm is left unfastened to show construction. She has a paper tag reading "Doll Made by Anna Margaret Sheldon Nee Chase". A rare feature is her snap-on bow, seen in the inset and the 1921 patent drawing. She is 16in (41cm) as is the doll standing on the far right (77.2876) which has classic short hair, stitched joints at elbows and knees and sateen covering the upper limbs and torso on which is written in script: "These dolls were orginated in 1890 by M. J. Chase, Elizabeth K. Chase, Anna M. Sheldon (daughter)"; c. 1910.

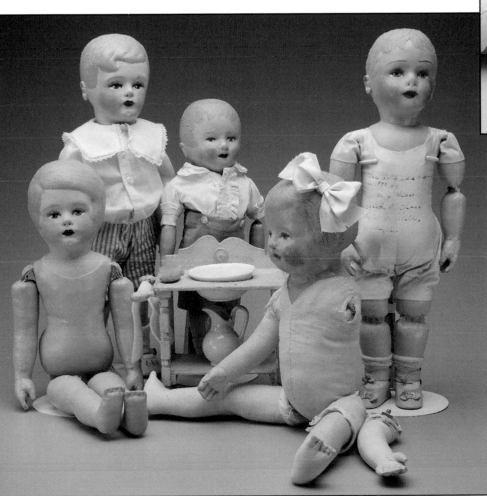

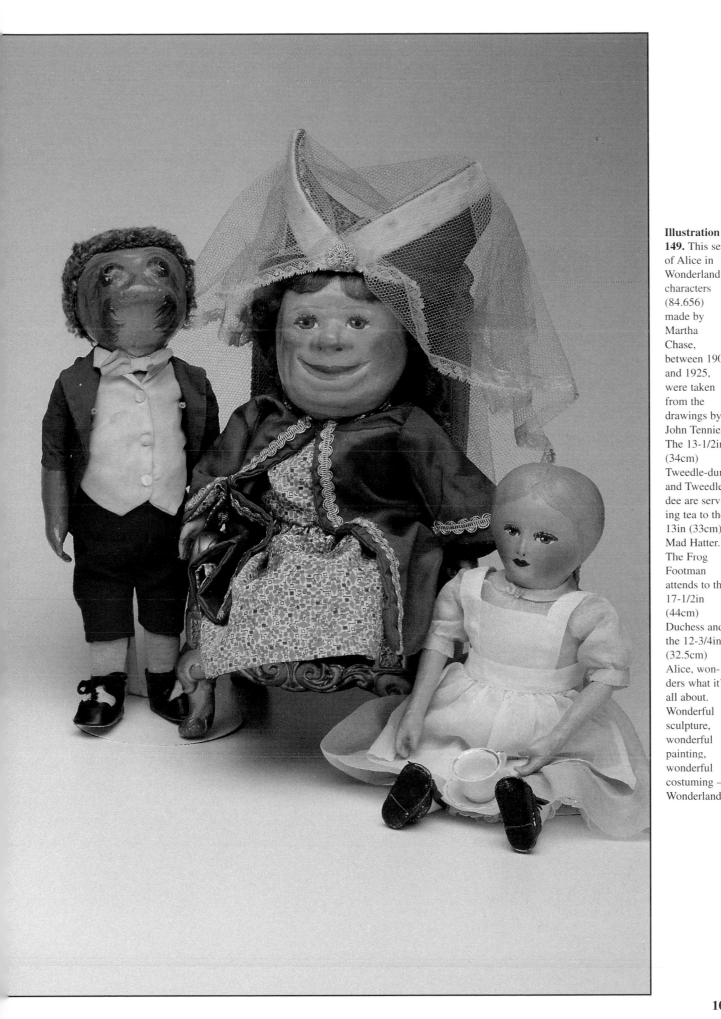

Illustration 149. This set of Alice in Wonderland characters (84.656) made by Martha Chase, between 1905 and 1925, were taken from the drawings by John Tenniel. The 13-1/2in (34cm) Tweedle-dum and Tweedle-dee are serving tea to the 13in (33cm) Mad Hatter. The Frog Footman attends to the 17-1/2in (44cm) Duchess and the 12-3/4in (32.5cm) Alice, wonders what it's all about. Wonderful sculpture, wonderful painting, wonderful costuming — Wonderland!

Top Left: **Illustration 150.** The Mad Hatter (84.656), 15in (38cm), with the molds from whence he came. Plaster and metal negatives are shown with a cloth positive. While several other Chase dolls were made using molds taken from bisque dolls of the period, the Mad Hatter is truly unique. *Top Right:* **Illustration 151.** These two dolls show interesting differences in paint color. The African-American (81.383) on the left has a sateen covered body and minimal hair painting. The larger doll's skin tone is a redder brown (81.386), ca 1905. It is referred to as "Indian Doll" on the box. They are 20 and 25in (51 and 63cm).

Illustration 152. Martha Chase's Little Nell (77.2874), ca 1910, inspired by the literature of Charles Dickens (center) is flanked by a gentleman (80.426), ca 1921, dressed in green and an undressed lady (77.2872), ca 1910, bearing the Chase Hospital Doll trademark.

Illustration 153. This portrayal of an African-American (77.2882), 28in (70cm), is full of warmth and character.

Illustration 154 . Proudly American stand these three; Martha Chase's George Washington (81.385), 25in (63.5cm) of solid strength, a 22in (56cm) Alabama Indestructible Doll (74.206) in stars and stripes and an 18in (46cm) 1916 Georgene Averill "Miss America" (76.1863) with a mask face and a music box which plays "My Country 'Tis of Thee Of Thee". Of thee we sing.

Illustration 155. A large, 18in (46cm) Philadelphia Baby (77.2888) and two Alabama babies (79.9784 and 79.9785), 12 and 14in (31 and 36cm) respectively, illustrate the work from other dollmakers of the period. The Philadelphia doll was distributed by the J.B.Sheppard & Co. from about 1900 to 1920; its maker's name remains unknown. Nicely painted, they are sculpted with a heavily defined edge around the eye and often deep mouth modeling. The elbows are not jointed but the hands and feet are nicely stitched. The two smaller dolls were made by Ella Smith of Roanoke, Alabama. She produced her "Alabama Babies" from 1904 to 1924. She obtained 5 patents for the production of her dolls, which were stuffed through the tops of their heads and have a circular pate stitched around the crown. A delightful short story by Richard Waller about Ella Smith and her factory appeared in the August 1993 *Doll Reader®*.

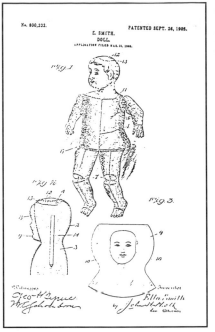

Illustration 156.
1905 E. Smith
Doll patent
details constuc-
tion techniques.

Illustration 157.
1922
E. L. Smith
patent for a
cloth cat.

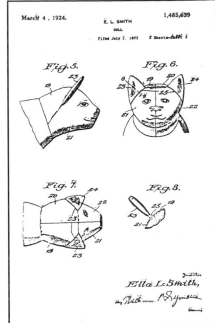

Illustration 158. Gertrude Rollinson's dolls were produced by the Utley Co. of Holyoke, Mass between 1916 and 1917, a short production period which makes them quite rare. They were produced in several sizes with painted hair or three different wig styles. Some are dolly-faced, like the 18-1/2in (47cm) wigged girl (79.9775). They are marked with a diamond-shaped stamp on the front of the torso. Some are very similar to the dolls of Martha Chase. An undressed Chase (81.390) stands in the middle for comparison with an undressed Rollinson (79.9774), both are 20in (51cm).

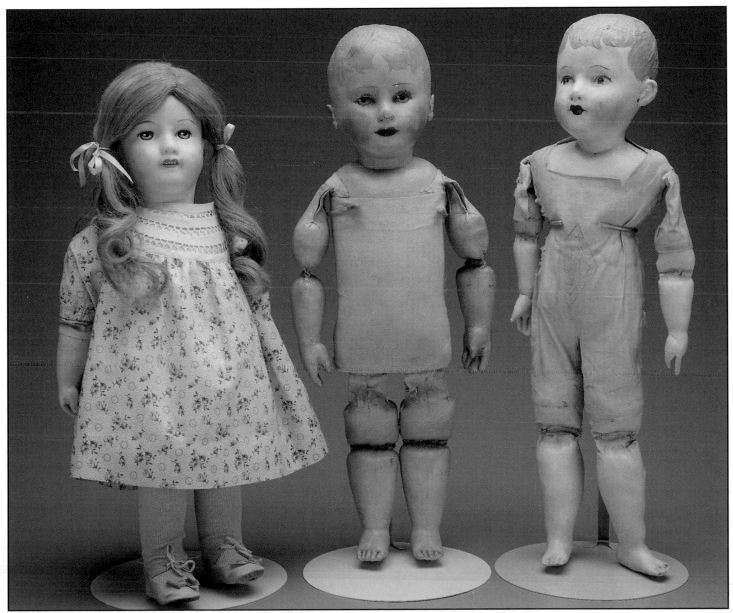

Illustration 159. Popular comic characters included the Katzenjammer Kids, from the comic strip by Rudolph Dirks. The 1925 Knickerbocker Toy Co's Fritz (80.4622), Captain (80.4621) and Hans (80.4620) are wonderful characters, 16 and 18in (42 and 46cm) tall. Nancy (74.188) and Sluggo (80.4619) were drawn by Ernie Bushmiller and produced in 1944 by Georgene Novelties. They are 14in (36cm) tall and as bright as the day they were made.

Illustration 160. Kamkins — A "Dolly to Love" was the trademark of the Louise R. Kampes Studio for the wonderful dolls sold at her shop on the Boardwalk at Atlantic City, New Jersey. What fond memories the shop held for little girls later in life, who describe clothing hanging on lines like washing, and who were able to choose a new outfit or two during their seaside vacations. This Kamkins, ca. 1920, is 19in (48cm), with a hand-painted face, human hair wig and swing joints. She retains her red paper heart sticker on her chest as well as a wonderful wardrobe of original clothes. *Darlene J. Gengelbach Collection.*

Illustration 161. Dolly Dollykins (79.439) and Bobby Bobbykins (79.438), were trademarks registered by Frank A. Hays, whose company was the Children's Novelty Co. These cute round-faced, round-eyed dolls share a kinship with Grace Drayton's Campbell kids, as her sister Margaret was also a published illustrator with a style similar to Grace's, who married Mr. Hays... Likely a family endeavor, these dolls appeared only in 1909-1910. This tiny pair is only 7in (18cm) tall. They are seen with another popular imp of the era, the Kewpie (78.1111), who was made in several styles in cloth. Distributed through George Borgfeldt, this Kewpie is 15in (38cm), late 1920s.

Illustration 162. Cloth dolls were manufactured by the Alexander Doll Company from the time it was founded in 1923. The girl in white (80.5108) with the blond Dutch bob and side-glancing eyes is 19-1/2in (49cm). She looks like many of the comic strip characters of the 1930s from when she dates, but her tag only records, "Created by Mme Alexander NY." The small doll with the yarn hair in front is a World War II baby, a 14-1/2in (37cm) Little Shaver (76.348). Elsie Shaver was an illustrator of Victorian children from whom Madame Alexander had bought reproduction rights; the Shaver dolls maintained popularity for 20 years. Seen with the Alexanders is a 21in (53cm) sloe-eyed young lady made by Etta Kidd and her all-woman company in New York City, 1927-30. The quality of this eyelashed doll is excellent, and her clothes are nicely labeled. *Etta doll courtesy of Dorothy McGonagle.*

Illustration 163. The art of Maude Tousey Fangel gently holds "Sweets" (84.437), a cloth doll of her design from 1938. Manufactured by Georgene Novelties, the sweet doll is 14-1/2in (37cm).

Left: **Illustration 164.** Throughout the last decades of the 20th century many little girls were enchanted by the 10in (25cm) Hollie Hobbie (93.362) and the 18-1/2in (47cm) Strawberry Shortcake (94.617), simple little faces, sweet little girl dolls with whom they shared companionship. They have already achieved a nostalgia for many who played with them then and are mothers of little girls now. Another charming baby doll is seen, the 46cm Georgene doll, "Teardrop Baby" (97.8889), done from a design by noted Rochester, New York painter and doll artist, Diane Dengel. *Below:* **Illustration 165.** From the prolific Georgene Novelties, Inc. workshops came these three cloth characters, all still retaining their paper tags. The 18-1/2in (47.5cm) Uncle Wiggly (80.1970) from the stories by Howard R. Garis, 1943; the 18in (46cm), ever-popular Raggedy Andy (77.3247) by Johnny Gruelle, 1951 and the 13in (33cm), feather-brained Becassine (80.1971) with a label that reads "Paris Amie Desenfants-Children's Favorite, Copr 1953 Editions Gautierlanguereau." Becassine has been called France's Raggedy Ann, a tribute to her good-heartedness and her longevity.

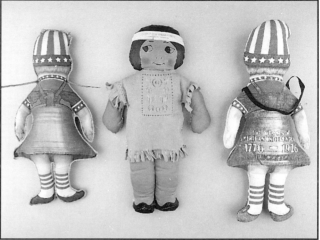

Illustration 166. Three printed American cloth dolls from throughout the century include the 1926 Annin & Co Liberty Belle (76.893) 13 1/2in (35cm), celebrating 150 years of American Independence on the left, and the Middle Falls Toy Works 1976 version on the right (76.905) 15-3/4in (39cm), honoring 200 years. They flank a 1933 Little Miss Chicago Century of Progress (75.5519) 14in (36cm). All depicted front and back.

Illustration 167. Back view of *Illustration 165*.

Illustration 168. A spread of Raggedy Ann and Andy dolls covering a mantel at the Concord Museum in Massachusetts. They also cover the entire production of Johnny Gruelle's beloved Raggedy, from the left, the earliest hand-made Ann, a cat, and Andy on the left from P.F. Volland; a Molly'es Ann; McCall's Patterns homemade Andy and pair; Georgene Novelties' awake/asleep, Beloved Belindy and pair; Knickerbocker's 1960s versions; and a Hasbro Playskool 1987 Ann. A visual treat, they affirm the continuous appeal to American children of this simple icon. *Photo by Dorothy McGonagle,* with permission of Concord Museum, Concord, MA. Dolls loaned from several collections; early Vollands from *Rebecca Mucchetti Collection.*

20ᵀᴴ CENTURY COMPOSITION

In the never-ending search for inexpensive, durable materials from which to make dolls' heads and parts, sawdust and glue in combination with various other materials seemed a natural candidate. American dollmakers surely had plentiful supplies of sawdust from the mills of our expanding nation and hide glue from the meat processing plants in Kansas City and Chicago at the turn of this century. There were three different methods — cold poured, cold pressed or hot pressed — variously in use from about 1910 until the late 1940s. Initially, the material, consisting primarily of clay pulp, was mixed and either poured or pressed cold into one part molds which were slow drying. Later, steam was used to compress the wood pulp mass between two part metal molds

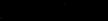

Illustration 169. Photographs from within the Averill Manufacturing Company show women at work putting on the wigs and men spraying the doll parts inside paint drums. Photos are part of an album maintained by an Averill Company salesman, now in the Strong Museum library, ca 1920.

in a process called hot pressing which took 30 minutes to dry, thus increasing production. The finished part consisted of two pieces which were then glued together. The end-product was good, competition among American manufacturers was brisk, and the result was that the manufacture of American-made dolls exceeded the numbers of imported dolls for the first time in 1910. Off and running, the composition doll business in America generated a broad range of artistic and innovative designs such as Billiken (*illustration 21*) noted in the historical perspective. The production process was very well established by the time importation of German goods was curtailed in 1916-1918. Composition dolls held sway until the development of inexpensive plastics during World War II. A vast number of companies produced or assembled composition dolls in America. Some of the giants were Alexander, Amberg, Arranbee, Averill, Cameo, Effanbee, Horsman and Ideal; many small businesses also produced beautiful American composition dolls. They have left substantial records which have enabled today's researchers to provide encyclopedic coverage of their operations, productions, designers and business relationships. This sampling of dolls from the Strong Museum collection illustrates the scope and variety of these very American dolls.

Illustration 170. Georgene Averill Native American baby (80.4687) has composition swivel head with painted features and hair. Strapped to a cradle board and dressed in brightly colored felt clothing, it measures 18in (46cm) overall, 1916.

Illustration 171. Pair of composition Skookum Indian dolls (87.1962 and 87.1963) designed by Mary McAboy, manufactured by H.H.Tammen Co. ca 1932, 14in (36cm) tall. The bodies are cloth over a stick of wood, and the dolls wear flannel blankets. The name "Skookum" is Siwash for "Bully Good" and was chosen fondly for the men and women McAboy had known. The dolls were originally made with apples for heads which did not age well, so composition was then used, but concurrently with the appleheads which some people preferred. By the 1920s, Skookums were being used in schools for educational purposes.

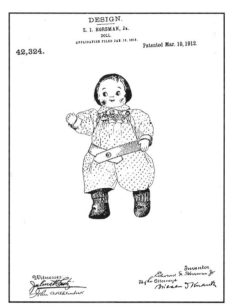

Illustration 172. Four pages in lovely hand-tinted colors from the Averill photo album show a variety of dolls offered, including Lullabye Baby and several sizes of Mama Dolls with cotton or silk dresses. Georgene Averill patented her cloth mama body with its loose hip joints and composition lower limbs on June 11, 1918. Creatively marketed through artistic window displays and by salegirls dressed as nurses teaching dolls to walk and talk, the mama dolls became the mainstay of the Averill line in the 1920s.

Illustration 173. 1912
E. I. Horsman, Jr. patent.

Illustration 174. 1912
E. I. Horsman, Jr. patent.

Illustration 175. Three composition dolls with ties to advertising include the 13in (33cm), ca. 1910 Campbell Kid (74.189) designed by Grace Drayton, associated for decades with soup. The label on the cuff of the 15in (38cm), Uneeda Kid's raincoat (73.1354) tells his story, "Uneeda Biscuit / Pat'd Dec. *, 1914 / Mfd. by Ideal Novelty & Toy Co." He guards his miniature box of biscuits. The African-American, 12in (31cm) Buddy Lee is Black Magic, Railroad Engineer (80.1919). He is the trademark doll for Lee jeans and his label, sewn on the back reads "Union made / Lee Reg. / U.S. Pat.Off." He dates from 1920.

Left: **Illustration 176.** In the style of traditional German bisque dolls come three American-made dolls. On the left, an 18in (46cm) girl incised Yankee Doll (80.5022), made by the Mitred Box Co of New York City and distributed through McClurg & Keen, 1911-13. She has painted blue eyes and a good quality jointed body. The large doll with sleep eyes stands 24in (61cm) and is stamped on her body Nedco Doll (79.9658), for the New England Doll Co of Holyoke, Mass., 1919-21. The 14in (36cm) baby doll (79.9667) is embossed Art Craft N.Y.C. on her head, has sleep eyes and was made between 1918-1920. They are all nice examples of American technology and materials producing a familiar feeling doll.

Below: **Illustration 177.** Boys just want to have fun — most of the time. The 11in (28cm) Velocipede Kid (79.9558), 1915, is from E.I.Horsman. His brown painted head has side-glancing eyes and a delightful smile. His feet are fastened to the front wheel and move up and down when pulled. Sitting in the 1930s wooden touring car is George McManus' Snookums (80.1116), the Newlywed's Baby as drawn from cartoons; note the resemblance to McManus' Maggie and Jiggs. He was sold by Aetna Doll & Toy, and is 11in (28cm), ca 1910. Ideal's Liberty Boy (74.161) is 12in (30.5cm) and represents a U.S. doughboy with molded uniform; he is a 1918 precursor to G.I. Joe, and is but one of a flood of patriotic dolls that appeared before and during World War I. The smiling African-American boy is Snowball (74.169); the tag on his sleeve reads, "Gene Carr Kids / from New York World's Lady / Bountiful Comic Series / Mfg by E.I.Horsman Co, N.Y." He dates from 1915 and is 13in (33cm). The 14-1/2in (37cm) Baby Grumpy (80.4951) from Fleischaker & Baum, 1924, apparently takes no comfort in knowing he is of fine quality.

Illustration 178. Three fabulous doll people show the detail and quality of fine sculpture transformed into composition dolls. The seated character is actor John Bunny (76.862) 13-1/2in (33.5cm), copyrighted by Louis Amberg and Son, 1914. They also manufactured the unmistakable Charlie Chaplin (74.172), 14in (36cm), who keeps his eye on the Spirit of Hollywood camera. The larger doll is the Raggedy Man (78.389) 15-1/2in (39cm), from the poem by James Whitcomb Riley. The doll was manufactured by E.I.Horsman, 1916, and the label notes the trademark was under license from L.P. Tucker. Original and in fine condition, all three retain their labels.

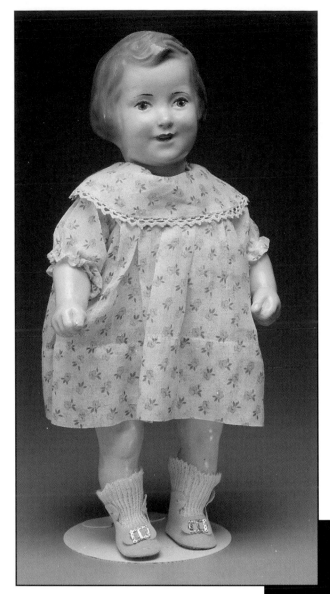

Illustration 179. Girl with molded side part hair (79.11126), 13in (33cm), is from Jessie McCutcheon Raleigh, designer and business woman whose initial success was a figurine named "The Good Fairy". Raleigh operated a successful doll business in Chicago from 1916-1920. She offered over forty models, for which she had hired the talents of artistic sculptors. Raleigh researched compositions and paint to produce dolls of excellent quality, some of the finest of the period. In 1920, she sold her business to the Pollyanna Co.

Illustration 180. Dolls signed Mrs. P.D. Smith are very rare and of compelling sculpture. Mabel and Putnam David Smith, along with their daughter Margaret, started a doll business in 1913. Because Mabel was a portrait artist, her early dolls are extraordinarily beautiful and lifelike. Working first out of their home in Santa Cruz, California, they created heads from a fine quality wood pulp composition. Their sculpting and painting was far superior to the handcrafted Munich Art Dolls of the same period, which had fostered the character doll movement in Germany. Apparently the Smiths initially adapted existing bodies of cloth, some with composition limbs and also German jointed bodies for their heads; later bodies had more uniformity. Some dolls had sleeping and flirting eyes, as does this 21-1/2in (55cm) dimpled girl with the big smile and painted teeth (77.697). Her socket head is mounted on a deep composition shoulderplate, her arms and legs are composition. The Smith distributor built a factory for more efficient production of the dolls in San Francisco in 1918, and although the dolls remained expensive, the quality declined and competition forced closure in 1922.

Illustration 181. Closeup of doll shown in *Illustration 179*.

Illustration 182. "Our Lindy" (75.5533) ca. 1928, aviator and hero from Regal Doll Co was sculpted by E. Peruggi. He has molded hair and painted features, a good likeness, cloth body and authentic flight suit. At 28in (71cm) he cuts an impressive figure, flying the friendly skies on his painted wood eagle, whose outstretched wings serve as steering handles. This unusual kiddie car (75.915) was made by S.A. Smith Mfg. Co of Brattleboro, VT, early 20th century.

Illustration 183. All from different manufacturers, these five prove that all babies don't look alike. From left to right they are Ideal's Tickle Toes (80.4948) with flirty eyes and lashes from around 1929 to 1934; Cameo Doll Co's 1924 Bye-lo Baby (74.170) by Grace Storey Putnam; the 1924 Lullabye Baby (79.11114) from Madame Hendren of Averill Manufacturing Co; the ca. 1930 Lamkin (77.7771), a new playmate from Effanbee and a 1927 Baby Dimples (85.9395) from E.I. Horsman. All have cloth bodies and molded hair. Note the distinctive chunky fisted hand of Lamkin, who also has an original pillow. These range in size from 13 to 17in (33-43cm). The bottle sterilizer would be kept busy with this group!

Illustration 184. Rose O'Neill's prolific pen produced charmingly impish and kindly characters, notably Kewpies and Scootles, who appeared in three dimensional forms from dolls to door knockers. Here the two small Kewpies (78.1123 and 78.1124), 7in (18cm) are powder shakers with perforated caps on back of heads. The larger dolls are a dressed, 12in (31cm) Scootles (78.1113) with painted features, curly hair, eyes looking to the right, and a body with joints at neck, arms and hips. The 11-1/2in (30cm) black Kewpie (77.3254) is jointed only at the arms. The larger undressed, 12in (31cm) Kewpie (78.1119) is completely jointed — legs, arms and head — and is a rare sleeping eyed Kewpie. The three large dolls are from the Cameo Doll Products Co. of Joseph P. Kallus, who maintained a lifelong friendship with Rose O'Neill. The April 1989 issue of *Doll Reader*® contains several articles celebrating the legendary Kewpies and their inspired creator.

Illustration 185. From the realm of entertainment Amberg produced this doll 19-1/2in (49cm) of child star Baby Peggy (80.4953), 1923, sold through Sears, Roebuck & Co. She has a molded short page-boy styled hairdo and a memorable smile. The 17-1/2in (45cm), Horsman Ella Cinders (79.11130), 1925, is from the comic strip by Bill Counselman and Charlie Plumb which tells a rags to riches story. Effanbee's 14in (35.5cm) Skippy (80.1383), 1929, was originally from a comic strip by Percy L. Crosby made into a movie character played by Jackie Cooper, so Skippy covers both sources. All have cloth bodies with composition limbs.

Illustration 186. Strongly modeled and well-made dolls from Louis Amberg include the 13-1/2in (35cm) girl on the left (79.9672) in the sailor suit from ca. 1928, and second from the right, the ca. 1923 Mibs (79.11127), who is 16in (41cm) tall. She is a "Phyllis May" doll, designed by Hazel Drucker and has distinctive red hair. Even more singular is the orange hair of the 13-1/2in (35cm) Sunny Orange Blossom (79.9669), from 1924 on the far right. whose cap is in the form of a dimpled orange. The smaller doll, 12-1/2in (32cm) is a whistling boy (80.4952) from the Averill Manufacturing Co, 1929.

Illustration 187. Through the 1930s, the movies provided entertainment and escape and a continuing source of inspiration for the dollmakers, as this group of celebrity dolls illustrates. On the left, Madame Alexander's 1939 Scarlett O'Hara (79.318), 14-1/2in (37cm), a ca. 1935 Shirley Temple look-alike (80.5207) in a Hawaiian outfit, who represents Marama, from the movie "The Hurricane". 12in (30cm), Effanbee's 1930 W.C. Fields (73.1899) with ventriloquist dummy mechanism, 18in (46cm) and a 22in (56cm) Effanbee Anne Shirley (79.323) from 1936, whose marked body style was also used for the Dewees Cochran American Children series.

Illustration 188. Among other movie stars who were created in doll form are Madame Alexander's 1937 Jane Withers (84.458), 17in (43cm) who is modeled with the actress's character and who retains her 1937 price tag from Sears, Roebuck & Co. of $4.29. Beside her stands skating star Sonja Henie (80.4929), from ca. 1939, also by Madame Alexander, who is 14in (36cm). The tall doll is a 25in (63cm), ca. 1938, Ideal Deanna Durbin (80.1031), while Effanbee's Charlie McCarthy (74.619) 20-1/2in (52cm), c. 1938, sits at her feet.

Above Left: **Illustration 189.** Ideal's ca. 1934 Shirley Temple (73.424) in 11in (28cm) size, in original pleated pink dress. *Right:* **Illustration 190.** Two religious sects of longstanding historical interest are depicted by these mid 1930s dolls. On the left, a Shaker (87.1959) with a blonde mohair wig wears a simple lavender-red dress and triangular shawl. The Amish girl (85.4742) retains a paper label on her arm: Pennsylvania Dutch Dolls by Marie Polack Reg U.S. Pat Off. The doll is an Effanbee Baby Grumpy doll, and the costuming has good detail. They are 12 and 13in (31 and 33cm).

Illustration 191. Little Orphan Annie (73.1352), the plucky heroine from the Harold Gray comic strip is 12in (30.5cm) and is seen with her dog Sandy (73.1355), a cute pup. They were manufactured by Freundlich in the 1930s. Seen with them is the 10-1/2in (26cm) swashbuckling cat Puss-in-boots (80.1947), ca 1930, with jointed limbs and swivel head.

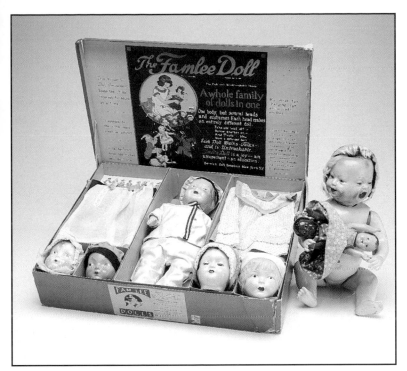

Illustration 192. Multiple dolls in three forms include The Famlee Doll (80.425) by the Berwick Doll Co., 40.5cm, 1921. "A whole family of dolls at once", the four extra heads screw onto the body and came boxed with several appropriate outfits. A 13-1/2in (35cm), multi-face baby (78.1033), ca. 1930 is seated to the right, its four faces are smiling, sleeping, yawning and crying, of which two are most visible. A cardboard hood covers the head and faces are turned by pressing a metal bar on the front of the torso. This baby holds a 7-1/2in (19cm) topsy-turvy doll with one head African-American and one Caucasian, both with painted features, ca. 1935.

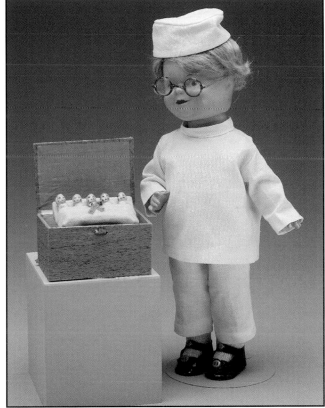

Illustration 193. The May 28, 1934 birth of the Dionne Quintuplets in Callander, Ontario, Canada became a media event of astonishing proportion. A miracle of survival, their every moment was documented for a public whose interest in these five little girls was insatiable. Marketing opportunities abounded; doll companies enjoyed the concept of selling five dolls at once, but it was the Alexander Doll Co of New York who was granted the rights to the name Dionne Quintuplets. These two sets are the 7in (18cm) 1935 bent limb babies (77.3253) with molded hair and painted eyes seated in a wooden multiple playpen, along with the 1936 toddler version (81.1006 to 81.1010), 14in (36cm), standing behind. These have sleep eyes and dark brown curled human hair wigs. As the girls grew, they were observed at play by paying tourists and they endured lengthy hair styling sessions each day. Each doll is identified by clothing color: Marie in blue, Emilie in lavender, Cecile in green, Annette in yellow and Yvonne in pink.

Illustration 194. Dr. Allan Roy Dafoe (80.1990), who attended the quints birth and managed their subsequent care was part of Alexander's offerings. He has a grey mohair wig, painted features, and wears surgical clothes. He is 13-1/2in (34cm), dates from around 1936, and is shown with a boxed set of tiny quintuplets (80.1595) marked on the lid The Callander Miracle, probably an early souvenir item.

Illustration 195. Effanbee's Patsy was introduced in 1928 and met with immediate approval. Like many other dolls, she was designed by Bernard Lipfert, a master designer of dolls faces and figures for the American industry from the time he emigrated in 1912 from Germany. Character dolls artistically made in a faithful likeness of celebrities maintained a special place, but were balanced by dolls with the effect of a lifelike child, but with eyes widened, cheeks plumped and tiny mouths like a rosebud...like Patsy. Appealing and comfortable, Patsy was a wonderful playmate, one a child could keep company with for years, as many did. The Schoenhut Company saw the appeal of Patsy, and in its final year of producing dolls, 1935, made a composition child much in her image, which emulates Patsy's wistful expression and her bent right arm. Patsy (74.207) is 14in (36cm) and the Schoenhut (84.149) is 13in (33cm).

Illustration 196. This group of dolls from the 1930s includes two 7in (18cm) Tiny Betty dolls based on literary characters, a theme often seen in dolls from Madame Alexander. These represent Jo (80.1994) from Louisa May Alcott's Little Women and Charles Dicken's David Copperfield (80.1996). A 19in (49cm) Patsy Ann (80.1384), part of the growing Patsy family from Effanbee holds a 10-1/2in (26.5cm) Patsy Baby Kin (77.3245), still wearing her metal heart bracelet. A Vogue doll from 1940 (80.1961), 7-1/2in (19cm), dressed in a regional costume completes the group.

Illustration 197. Dewees Cochran's designs for American Children were adapted by Effanbee for production in composition from 1936 to 1939. Graceful and natural-looking, they show a subtle blend of idealism and realism in their sculpture and painting. The eyes are particularly expressive and beautifully painted; the dolls also came with sleep eyes. Both have the distinctive Anne Shirley body. The brown eyed, 20in (50.7cm) tall girl is dressed like a typical American child (79.10657), and the blue eyed, 21-1/8in (53.3cm) tall girl as a Red Cross nurse (81.279). By the late 1930s a new wave of patriotism and service was being felt in America.

Illustration 198. These three baby dolls span the decade from 1930 to 1940, and show three different influences on dollmakers. Baby Sandy (80.4954) of the movies inspired Freundlich's cute little 8in (20cm) all-composition character, the 11in (28cm) Horsman Company's baby (79.351) on a classic cloth Mama body with composition arms is from the realm of advertising. His label reads: Mellin's Food Doll Boston, Mass. From Georgene Novelties, Inc.'s "True to Life" line comes the 21in (53cm) Baby Yawn (77.3249).

Illustration 199. The 1941-51 Monica Studios doll (76.345) by Mrs. Hansi Share is unusual in that she has human hair rooted into the composition instead of a glued-on wig. She is a young woman of her time; her distinctly red lips are indicative of the forties, as is her pulled back hairstyle. She is 20in (51cm) tall.

Illustration 200. During the Second World War, the Freundlich Novelty Corporation produced several fine dolls honoring those who served. General Douglas MacArthur (74.181), "The Man of the Hour", is 18in (46cm) of true-to-life detail in both modeling and uniform. Servicemen from all branches were depict-ed. In 1942 Congress authorized the establishment of women's noncombatant branches of the service; and they too were honored with dolls in their likeness-es. Seen are a WAAC, Women's Auxiliary Army Corp (80.1952), and a WAVE, a Navy adjunct (74.182), both 15in (39cm) tall.

HARD PLASTIC AND VINYL

Plastic is a development of modern synthetic resins made from natural sources such as coal, limestone, petroleum, salt and water.

Through the magic of modern chemistry, we now have an endless variety of man-made plastic materials with qualities for every purpose. Fifty years and more have shown that dolls and toys of plastic are expanding in quality and variety. A perspective on this is that the collector's beloved bisque dolls were in fact produced worldwide for not much more than 60 years. Plastic has the versatility to expand as rapidly as our everchanging lifestyles as we proceed into the 21st century. The Strong Museum has been acquiring examples from these latest decades which reflect American culture and modern history.

1940s

Illustration 201. The 1940s saw the introduction of hard plastic for dolls, though other materials continued to be used, notably composition and rubber. Sometimes heads and bodies were of different materials. The two babies on the left demonstrate this variety; the Sun Rubber Company baby, Sunbabe (80.4731), ca. 1950, 10in (25cm) is all rubber, but is included to show its similarity to the Ideal Company's Betsy Wetsy (89.980), 12in (30cm), who was introduced in 1937 as a concept of true life dolls, and in competition with Effanbee's Dy-Dee baby. Drink and wet babies served a teaching purpose; baby dolls remained popular throughout the forties, and many children helped their mothers care for younger siblings or through doll play gained an understanding of the responsibility that childcare involved. This Betsy dates from 1948, and has hard plastic head and rubber body. Two old favorites that were later released in vinyl include the 25in (63cm) Georgene Averill doll (81.1074), ca. 1945, and Grace Storey Putnam's Bye-lo baby (79.9758), 15in (38cm), ca. 1940 released through George Borgfeldt & Co.

Illustration 202. Mary Hoyer (81.1013), 14-1/2in (36cm) wears a knitted outfit. She was made by the Mary Hoyer Doll Mfg Co of Reading Pa., ca. 1945. The ca. 1950 Ideal Toni doll (80.366), 14in (35cm) has a nylon wig and came with a home permanent kit. Both are hard plastic.

Illustration 203. By the 1950s the influence of television was being felt strongly in the doll world. Hopalong Cassidy (80.4673) is but one character produced in doll form, vinyl head and cloth body, 21in (53cm) from Ideal, ca. 1949. Westerns were big, all boys were "into" cowboys, and girls often followed suit, as seen by 16in Terri Lee (80.4944), ca. 1950. From the field of entertainment, the 1955 Emmett Kelly (77.2334) as Willie the Clown in vinyl with a cloth body was made by the Baby Barry Toy Co. of New York, 21-1/2in (54cm) tall.

Illustration 204. The 1950s saw a great interest in the 7 to 8in (18 to 20cm) hard plastic jointed dolls, often with walking legs and sleep eyes. This group includes, front, 1952 Muffie (78.238) from the Nancy Ann Storybook Co with walking legs and her original box, two 1954 Vogue Ginny dolls, a cowgirl (80.369) and a roller skater (80.370) dressed in typical 1950s casual style, and Davy Crockett (80.5194), another Storybook doll. Seated on the bench are a 1954 Vogue Ginny (80.203) in a hat and a dress to match, an Alexander Doll Co. infant called "Little Genius" (80.4910) from 1957 who is the only vinyl doll in the group, and lastly, 1957 Jill (80.4937), Ginny's big sister, 10in (25.5cm).

Illustration 205. Poor Pitiful Pearl (80.4947) captured the heart of many a young girl who wanted to adopt the 17in (43cm) needy waif, designed by cartoonist William Steig, from a series he did for the New Yorker called "Small Fry." Produced by Glad Toy Co. in the mid 1950s, Pearl was sold with adoption papers and a pretty dress with which the new adoptive "mother" could transform Pearl to something closer to a princess, but Pearl remains in the public mind as Poor and Pitiful. Beside her stands a ca. 1950 Nanette (80.4933), 14-1/2in (37cm) from the R & B (Arranbee) Doll Co of New York, a stylish young girl. Dress-up was important as 9in (23.5cm), ca. 1950 Cissette (80.1983) from Madame Alexander illustrates, but truly marking the dateline is the Sun Rubber Co. vinyl 12in (31cm) doll with molded hair and hat (77.2569) who could be none other than an entertaining Mouseketeer from the popular 1950s television show.

Illustration 206. The Littlechap Family from Remco Industries, 1963, included 14-1/2in (37cm) tall Dr. John (79.11121), his 14-1/2in (37cm) (including hair) wife Lisa (79.11122) and two daughters 13in (33cm) Judy (79.11123) and 10-1/2in (26cm) Libby (80.5208). A large wardrobe was offered as well as a doctor's office and various rooms and furniture, which folded up into a carrying case. Detailed identities came with each and group activities stressed family values.

Illustration 207. Four 1960s dolls inspired from literature, cartoons, and current events. The large doll is Madame Alexander's 1961 Jacqueline Kennedy (80.1980), vinyl head on hard plastic body, 20in (51cm) of elegance and style. Instantly recognizable, the ca. 1960 Charlie Brown (80.1282), Charles M. Schulz comic creation, was an immediate American success and remains popular today. Mary Poppins (80.1963), ca. 1964, Horsman dolls, from the Disney movie which brought P.L. Travers' magical English nanny to life in a 12in (30cm) doll, while the ca. 1965, 10-1/2in (26cm) African-American boy (77.2887) from the Chase firm of Pawtucket Rhode Island shows that the work Martha Jenks Chase began in cloth 80 years earlier continued in vinyl. The company has since closed its doors.

Illustration 208. In 1964 Madame Alexander offered these 7-1/2in (19cm) vinyl head/plastic body Quintuplets (81.1011), unofficially representing the Fisher Quints, who were born in the fall of 1963.

Illustration 209. "When Barbie Dated G.I.Joe" was the title of an exhibit at the Strong Museum that explored "America's Romance with Cold War toys from 1945 to 1970". Apparently when this 1960, 11-1/2in (29cm) Barbie (80.4967) dated this ca. 1970 G.I. Joe (77.486), they went out on his motorcycle. Barbie®, Teen-Age Fashion Model Doll by Mattel was designed by Ruth Handler and premiered in 1959; she remains a phenomenon today. Joe was copyrighted by Hasbro, Inc. in 1964.

Illustration 210. Sweet uncomplicated play dolls that reflect the need for simplicity in the 1980s, are seen in Fisher-Price's 15-1/2in (39cm) vinyl girl doll from ca. 1980, "My Friend Mandy" (93.361), and Playskool's typically colorful, 22in (56cm), 1986 "My Buddy" (94.572). They have vinyl heads and cloth torsos. The continuing popularity of Sesame Street led to a profusion of their characters, including a 9in (23cm) Ernie puppet (94.621), from ca. 1985. Made by Playskool Baby, Inc. is the 5in (12.5cm) little Big Bird (93.1683) from 1993, who brightened some many days. Ernie and Big Bird are trdemark characters of Jim Henson Productions.

Illustration 211. The movies provided constant inspiration not only for doll manufacturers; Marilyn Monroe (83.351), movie star and icon caught the imagination of many. This 1983 vinyl Marilyn is 18in (46cm) and from the World Doll Co, Inc.

Illustration 212. A few dolls of the 1990s reflect a diverse cross-section of American doll production and influences. The distinctive Bart Simpson (92.854) acknowledges the mischievous television character, while the African-American 11-1/2in (29cm) Barbie (94.836), from 1994, acknowledges cultural diversity. The 10-1/2in (26cm), "Happy to be Me" doll (93.558) represents a realistically proportioned young lady that contrasts with the idealized and unnatural proportions of Barbie's body. Cathy Mededig designed this doll for the High Self Esteem Toy Corp. A little McDonald's "Happy Meal" toy doll, 4in (9.5cm) (94.220) was a 1993 Christmas offering. Vogue celebrated the Girl Scouts 80th anniversary with 9in (23cm) Daisy (94.579), an African-American Ginny Doll from 1992.

Illustration 213. The Cabbage Patch dolls were first created in 1978 of sculptured cloth by Alabama dollmaker Xavier Roberts, as seen by the 1983, 23in (58cm) doll on the left, named Marian Luella (95.543). The vinyl versions, licensed in 1983, created a craze which swept the country. A pair of 17-1/2in (45cm) twin boys (95.533), from 1985, in original box are primarily for children, whereas the 1986, 17in (43c,m) Statue of Liberty Cabbage Patch doll (95.536) with a porcelain head is primarily for adult collectors.

Illustration 214. Claire Castle, a typical American child poses with her Pleasant Company American Girl doll, Samantha in 1995. The 18in (46cm) dolls represent various historical American periods — Samantha, the Victorian era. A series of books further the company's efforts toward education through entertainment.

ARTIST DOLLS

At one level or another, every doll reflects the artistry of its creator. Through the ages, many artists have turned to dollmaking to express their talents. Whatever the medium or level of talent involved, all dolls share the caring which brought the creative effort to fruition. Although the primary concern of this book is the play doll, a glimpse at a few fine artist dolls from the span of the 20th century gives a look at this aspect of the doll from within Strong Museum.

Illustration 215. In tribute to Strong Museum's founder, New York doll artist Jeanne Singer was engaged to create this 13in (33cm) portrait doll in bisque of Margaret Woodbury Strong (95.1137) as a bride in 1920. Working from the original wedding photographs, Singer rendered a fine image, 1982.

Illustration 216. Martha Thompson of Wellesley, Massachusetts deftly sculpted in bisque a stunning likeness of the beautiful American actress Grace Kelly (77.2669) in a miniaturized version of her 1956 wedding gown when she became Princess Grace of Monaco.

The fairy-tale wedding enchanted girls young and old alike. The 1957, 21in (53cm) doll is typical of Thompson's attention to detail. Thompson was a member of NIADA, the National Institute of American Doll Artists, an organization comprised of artists creating original work in a multitude of media.

Illustration 217. The sculptured needlework of Dorothy Wendell Heizer is without parallel. Miniscule stitches and an attention to detail are the hallmarks of the Essex Fells, New Jersey artist's great talent. At a mere 10in (25.7cm), the detail rendered in this 1955 portrayal of Vivien Leigh as Scarlett O'Hara (79.301) is remarkable. Could anyone but Scarlett wear green velvet drapery so well; could anyone but Heizer miniaturize it so superbly?

Illustration 218. This great group is the work of three noteworthy American artists. The 1961 Uncle Sam (76.1850) is an original portrait doll in wax by Lewis Sorenson. His face, so full of character, combines the classic features of Uncle Sam with a kindly aura unique to Sorenson. He stands 18in (46cm) tall. The two children are from the noted artist, Dewees Cochran. The 12-1/2in (35cm) girl in a blue pinafore (76.629) is a rare balsa wood example of a Cochran prototype from 1940. The other Cochran doll (80.5057), in a print dress, is a 12in (31cm) Angela Appleseed at age five, from 1952. This doll is part of Cochran's Grown-up series, in which dolls modeled after real children are portrayed at various ages from five to twenty. The ca. 1955 Eleanor Roosevelt doll (79.9056) is from the hands of one artist working at home who began by making dolls to illustrate her daughter's geography and history lessons, a hobby that grew into an extensive pageant of dolls. Evelyn Greene of Bangor, Maine drew on her training in art and history to create her composition figures which illustrate the history of costume from the dawn of civilization through the 1940s. Roosevelt, 21in (53cm) tall, a thoughtful and dignified presence, is one of Greene's many fine representations of historical American figures. This sampling of American artist dolls celebrates the spirit of the American people.

DOLLS — A NOTE ON PRESERVATION

by **Darlene Gengelbach**, *Doll Conservator, Strong Museum*

Preservation. Conservation. Restoration. These terms are used extensively but loosely in the doll world today. But what does each really mean? And are they being used properly? It is time we addressed these questions. Let's begin by defining them precisely.

Preservation: The preventive action taken to halt or retard damage to or deterioration of an object by controlling its environment or by stabilizing its structure in order to maintain its aesthetic or historic integrity.

Conservation: The interventive action taken to treat damaged or deteriorating aspects of an object. Such treatments permit only a minimal impact on the doll's integrity and a minimal sacrifice of original material, while employing safely reversible methods and materials whenever and wherever possible. Conservation treatments are routinely accompanied by thorough written and photographic documentation—both "before" and "after".

Restoration: The restorative action taken to re-integrate a damaged or deteriorated aspect of an object both physically and visually. Missing or damaged parts can only be properly or ethically restored when what was once there is known or can be documented.

Through time dolls have been, and continue today, to be re-painted, re-wigged, re-dressed, and altered. Anything to "beautify" and make them more desirable to the collector seems permissible. Some dolls have been inappropriately sanded down and repainted, not for the sake of restoration but only to make them cleaner looking for display.

Regional dressed dolls were stripped of their original clothing, and dressed as cute little girls only because the exact same dolls in frilly clothing were more pleasing to the collector and were easier to sell. German bisque dolls have been taken out of their plain homespun clothing and, in order to compete with their more expensive French counterparts, redressed in fancy silk dresses with lots of lace. Until recently, these questionable actions were, more often than not, labeled as "restorations". Generally speaking, little or no attention was paid to the historical provenance of the dolls — the value that we are finally beginning to appreciate. They just had to look good.

In recent years there has appeared with encouraging frequency a number of doll conservation articles which express this concern. It seems that we are finally coming to realize the harm that has been done over the years, and are beginning to understand that the dolls of yesteryear are not, in a great many instances, just pretty things to play with and to show off to friends but are instead, documents of life and history that cannot be replaced and which must be preserved.

What can we do to ensure our children and grandchildren can enjoy the dolls we so cherish today? We can keep them as original as possible. We can always ask questions of the person we may be considering for repair work. What is his/her philosophy and ethical position with respect to the work needed? Can he/she provide references? We can make sure that we fully understand every detail of the work that is finally proposed—what impact will it have on the doll, now and in the future? We can be sure to request that any clothing, wigs, ect., that must be replaced be returned to us with the doll so that its original integrity can be preserved. By storing these separated pieces in a clearly labeled polyolefin plastic bag with the file on the doll, its future history will remain intact.

We can keep them safe. One of the safest places for your treasured dolls is in acid-free/chemically neutral (archival) boxes kept in a climate controlled environment — 50-70 F, 40-55% relative humidity, with no light. But we all want to see, enjoy, and share, our dolls. That's why we collect them. So what else can we do?

Many of us don't have a doll room to display our collection, nor can we necessarily afford light and humidity controlled glass cases. But what we can do is give our doll's the best conditions possible within our individual budgets. No matter where they are to be displayed, your dolls deserve the most you can do for them to assure their continued well being.

Perhaps the most critical but very controllable problem is light. There are three (3) types of lighting common to our homes.

1. Sunlight (natural) windows, glass doors, etc.,
2. Incandescent (artificial) common screw in bulbs,
3. Fluorescent (artificial) push in tubes.

All three can cause damage over time, but sunlight and fluorescent are by far, the worst culprits. Both emit considerable ultraviolet radiation (UV) which can quickly cause severe deterioration in the form of fading and embrittlement, in both natural (organic) and synthetic materials. The heat produced by any of the three sources, but especially by the incandescent types, can also lead to unwanted shrinkage problems.

Sunlight is easy to handle by covering windows and doors with room darkening shades or heavy draperies. Clear (or tinted) window films will block 95-100% of damaging light energy. So too will UV filtering Plexiglas. Fluorescent tubes can be fitted with filtering sleeves to remove the damaging UV. While the UV produced by an incandescent bulb can be said to be negligible, it should not be completely ignored. Over time, fading will occur. The heat produced by such sources is perhaps your most immediate concern—in a closed case, a significant temperature rise due to incandescent lighting can also be very detrimental. Never locate incandescent lights inside your display cases!

By keeping your dolls away from other heat (and dirt) sources—such as furnace ducts, and by making a serious effort to stabilize the relative humidity of their environment through the use of humidifiers and de-humidifiers, you will be significantly enhancing their state of preservation.

Always make sure that your dolls are securely fastened to structurally sound stands and that no bare metal is permitted to contact them or their clothing. Make sure too, that all shelving is secure, and that it stays that way by checking it regularly. Check "clothing hazards"—elastic in sleeves and panties, metal snaps and buttons, string tags, metal and painted jewelry, and bright clothing—regularly. These items, after a prolonged period of direct contact with a doll's "skin", can cause stains or may even become stuck due to common chemical reactions—most notably, oxidation, exacerbated by heat, and airborne moisture. Be especially careful with your vinyl dolls, as their skin seems to wick stains from a number of accessory and clothing types. Also, their "plastic" nature allows their form to be readily compressed, impressed, or deformed—possibly permanently—if carelessly positioned or stored.

Keep your dolls as clean as possible. Dust is very problematic. It attracts moisture to the surface of your dolls, catalyzing additional unwanted conditions. Keep any dust covers, especially plastic types, well-ventilated and well off the surface of your dolls. Many plastics off-gas chemicals which can react adversely with the materials of your dolls. Use only the polyolefin type. If your dolls are not in glass cases, drape sheer panel curtains over them when not being viewed/enjoyed. I like the sheer panels because you can see through them, thus facilitating their safer removal. Also, their light weight is less likely to disturb costumes and hair. Inspect all of your dolls and their clothing regularly for insect pests. An occasional vacuuming with a low powered vacuum and a synthetic mesh screen between the nozzle and the doll will help keep dust to a minimum.

Preventive maintenance will go a long way to insure a long life for your dolls. Remember that these fragile examples of the dolls of our ancestors can only look to you for their survival. You cannot rid yourselves of the agents of destruction but you can diminish their costly toll.

Darlene Gengelbach

SELECTED BIBLIOGRAPHY

Academic American Encyclopedia. Danbury, CT: Grolier, Inc., 1996

Anderton, Johana Gast. *The Collector's Encyclopedia of Cloth Dolls.* Lombard, IL: Wallace-Homestead Book Company, 1984.

_____. *Twentieth Century Dolls from Bisque to Vinyl.* North Kansas City, MO: The Trojan Press, 1971.

_____. *More Twentieth Century Dolls from Bisque to Vinyl.* North Kansas City, MO: Athena Publishing Co., 1974.

von Boehn, Max. *Dolls and Puppets.* London: George G. Harrap and Company, Ltd., 1932.

Bourcier, Paul G. and Formanek-Brunell, Miriam, *Dolls and Duty: Martha Chase and the Progressive Agenda.* Providence, RI: The Rhode Island Historical Society, 1989.

Bradshaw, Marjorie A. *The Doll House, Story of the Chase Doll.* Privately published, 1986.

Calvert, Karin; MacLeod, Anne Scott; et al, *A Century of Childhood,* 1820-1920 Rochester, New York: The Margaret Woodbury Strong Museum, 1984.

Campbell, Helen. *The American Girl's Home Book of Work and Play.* New York: G.P. Putnam's Sons, 1884.

Carruth, Gorton. *What Happened When.* New York: Signet, 1989.

Coleman, Dorothy S., Elizabeth Ann and Evelyn Jane. *The Age of Dolls.* Washington, D.C: Dorothy S. Coleman, 1965.

_____. *The Collector's Book of Dolls Clothes, Costumes in Miniature:* 1700-1929. New York: Crown Publishers, Inc., 1975.

_____. *The Collector's Encyclopedia of Dolls.* New York: Crown Publishers, Inc., 1968

_____. *The Collector's Encyclopedia of Dolls, Vol 2.* New York: Crown Publishers, Inc., 1986.

Corson, Carol. *Schoenhut Dolls.* Cumberland, MD: Hobby House Press, Inc., 1993.

Creevey, Caroline A. Stickney. *A Daughter of the Puritans.* New York, G.P. Putnam's Sons, The Knickerbocker Press, 1916.

Doll Collectors of America, Inc. *American Made Dolls and Figurines and Supplement, 1940, 1942; Doll Collector's Manuals,* 1946-1983.

Early, Alice K. *English Dolls, Effigies and Puppets.* London: B.T. Batsford, Ltd., 1955.

Encyclopaedia Britannica, 14th Edition. London, 1929-1939.

Encyclopedia Americana, Danbury, CT: Grolier, Inc., 1992.

Fawcett, Clara Hallard. *Dolls, A New Guide for Collectors.* Boston, Mass: Charles T. Branford, 1964.

_____. *Paper Dolls, A Guide to Costume.* New York: H. L. Lindquist Publications, 1951.

Formanek-Brunell, Miriam. *Made to Play House. Dolls and the Commercialization of American Girlhood, 1830-1930.* New Haven: Yale University Press, 1993.

Fox, Carl. *The Doll.* New York: Harry N. Abrams, Inc., 1973.

Fraser, Antonia. *Dolls.* New York: G. P. Putnam's Sons, 1963.

_____. *A History of Toys.* London: Delacorte Press, 1966.

Gandy, Thomas H. and Joan W. *Natchez Victorian Children, Photographic Portraits, 1865-1915.* Natchez: Myrtle Bank Press, 1981.

Gerken, Jo Elizabeth. *Wonderful Dolls of Papier Mache.* Lincoln, NE: Doll Research Associates, 1970.

Glubok, Shirley, *Home and Child Life in Colonial Days.* New York: Macmillan Publishing Co, Inc., 1969.

Golding, Amy Thomas. *Miniature Travelers.* Francestown, N.H.: Marshall Jones Company, 1956.

Hall, G. Stanley and Ellis, A. Caswell. *A Study of Dolls.* New York: E. L. Kellogg and Co., 1897.

Howard, Marian B. *Those Fascinating Paper Dolls.* New York: Dover Publications, Inc., 1981.

Izen, Judith. *Collector's Guide to Ideal Dolls.* Paducah, KY: Collector Books, 1994.

Jendrick, Barbara Whitton. *Antique Advertising Paper Dolls in Full Color.* New York: Dover, 1981.

Johl, Janet Pagter. *The Fascinating Story of Dolls.* New York: H. L. Lindquist, 1941.

_____. *More About Dolls.* New York: H. L. Lindquist, 1946.

_____. *Still More About Dolls.* New York: H. L. Lindquist, 1950.

_____. *Your Dolls and Mine.* New York: H. L. Lindquist, 1952.

King, Constance Eileen. The Collector's History of Dolls. New York: St. Martin's Press, 1978.

Larcom, Lucy. A New England Girlhood. Gloucester, Mass. Peter Smith, Corinth Books, Inc. 1961.

Lavitt, Wendy. *American Folk Dolls.* New York: Alfred A. Knopf, 1982.

_____. *Dolls, the Knopf Collectors' Guide to Antiques.* New York: Alfred A. Knopf, 1983.

McClintock, Inez and Marshall. *Toys in America.* Washington, D.C.: Public Affairs Press, 1961.

McClinton, Katharine Morrison. *Antiques of American Childhood.* New York: Bramhall House, 1970.

Mateaux, Clara L. *The Wonderland of Work.* New York: Cassell and Co. 1884.

Merrill, Madeline Osborne. *The Art of Dolls 1700-1940.* Cumberland, MD: Hobby House Press, 1985.

Musser, Cynthia Erfurt and McClelland, Joyce D. Precious Paper Dolls. Cumberland, MD: Hobby House Press, 1985.

Noble, John D. *Dolls.* New York: Walker and Co., 1967.

_____. *A Treasury of Beautiful Dolls.* New York: Hawthorn Books, Inc. 1971.

Perkins, Myla. *Black Dolls, 1820-1991.* Paducah, KY: Collector Books, 1993.

_____. *Black Dolls, Book II,* Paducah, KY: Collector Books, 1995.

Ryan, Mary. *Cradle of the Middle Class: The Family in Oneida County New York 1790-1865.* Cambridge University Press, 1981.

St. George, Eleanor. *The Dolls of Yesterday.* New York: Charles Scribner's Sons, 1948.

Trimpey, Alice Kent. *Becky, My First Love.* Baraboo, WI: Remington House, 1946.

Washburn, Dorothy. *Report, Preliminary Results, Doll Oral History Project,* Rochester, New York: Margaret Woodbury Strong Museum, 1988.

Whitton, Blair. *American Clockwork Toys 1862-1900.* Exton, Pa.: Schifter, 1981.

_____. *Paper Toys.* Cumberland, MD: Hobby House Press, 1986.

Whitton, Blair and Margaret. *Collector's Guide to Raphael Tuck & Sons.* Cumberland, MD: Hobby House Press, 1991.

World Book Encyclopedia, Chicago, Field Enterprises Educational Corp., 1977.

OTHER SOURCES

Doll Reader®
Antique Doll World
Dolls Magazine
Doll News, the Official Publication of the United Federation of Doll Clubs, Inc.
Sirocco Productions, Inc. Videos:
Raggedy Ann and Andy: Johnny Gruelle's Dolls with Hearts
The Doll Makers: Women Entrepreneurs, 1870 - 1940

INDEX

Illustration numbers appear in bold.